The Carriers $10-

The
Fourth
Man

The Fourth Man

The Reverend

Howard Moody
JUDSON MEMORIAL CHURCH
NEW YORK

THE MACMILLAN COMPANY, NEW YORK
COLLIER-MACMILLAN LIMITED, LONDON

First Printing

The Macmillan Company, New York
Collier-Macmillan Canada Ltd., Toronto, Ontario

Library of Congress catalog card number: 63-16116

Printed in the United States of America

ACKNOWLEDGMENTS

William Butler Yeats, "The Second Coming," from *Michael Robartes
and the Dancer*, copyright 1924 by The Macmillan Company.
Reprinted with the permission of The Macmillan Company.
Josef Lukl Hromadka, *Doom and Resurrection* (Richmond, Va.,
Madrus House, 1944), pp. 118–119.
From "Christmas 1940," by W. H. Auden. Reprinted from *The
Collected Poetry of W. H. Auden*, p. 119. Copyright 1945 by
W. H. Auden, by permission of Random House, Inc.
Seymour Krim, "Making It," *Views of a Nearsighted Cannoneer*
(New York, Excelsior Press Publishers, 1961), pp. 37–38. Re-
printed with permission of the author. Copyright 1961 by Sey-
mour Krim.
Antoine de Saint-Exupéry, *Wind, Sand and Stars* (New York,
Reynal and Hitchcock, 1939), p. 23. Copyright 1939 by Saint-
Exupéry, translated from the French by Lewis Galantière.
Richard N. Coe, *Eugene Ionesco* (New York, Grove Press, Inc.,
Evergreen Pilot Books, 1961), p. 13. Copyright 1961 by Richard
N. Coe and reprinted with permission of Grove Press, Inc.
Virgil Gheorghiu, "The Twenty-fifth Hour," from *Man Against Mass
Society*, by Gabriel Marcel (Chicago, Henry Regnery Company,
Gateway Books, 1962), p. 229.

Thomas Griffith, *Waist High Culture* (New York, Grosset and Dunlap, The Universal Library, 1959), pp. 207–208.

William Stringfellow, "Poverty, Piety, Charity and Mission," *The Christian Century*, Vol. 78, No. 19, May 10, 1961, p. 585. Reprinted with the permission of *The Christian Century*.

William H. Whyte, Jr., *The Organization Man* (New York, Doubleday Anchor, 1956), p. 16.

From quote appearing in "Heading into Space," by Dan Wakefield, *The Nation*, Vol. 187, No. 19, December 6, 1958, p. 424.

Rainer Maria Rilke, *Duino Elegies*, translated by C. F. MacIntyre (Berkeley, University of California Press, 1961), p. 57. Copyright by C. F. MacIntyre and reprinted with his permission.

C. S. Lewis, *Perelandra* (New York, The Macmillan Company, 1958), p. 81.

Eric Sevareid, "The Dark of the Moon," *The Reporter*, Vol. 18, No. 8, April 17, 1958, p. 4. Copyright 1958 by The Reporter Magazine, Inc. Reprinted by permission of Harold Matson Company, Inc.

Antoine de Saint-Exupéry, *Flight to Arras*, translated from the French by Lewis Galantière (New York, Reynal and Hitchcock, 1942), p. 113.

Lewis Mumford, *The Conduct of Life* (New York, Harcourt, Brace and Company, 1951), p. 253.

Rollo May, *Man's Search for Himself* (New York, W. W. Norton and Company, 1953), p. 257.

Morton and Lucia White, "The American Intellectual Versus the City," *The Future Metropolis* (New York, George Braziller, 1961), p. 214.

Lewis Mumford, *The City in History* (New York, Harcourt, Brace and World, Inc., 1961), p. 575.

Jane Jacobs, *The Life and Death of Great American Cities* (New York, Random House, 1961), p. 436.

T. S. Eliot, from "Choruses from 'The Rock,'" *Collected Poems 1909–1935* (New York, Harcourt, Brace and World, Inc., 1936), p. 103. Copyright by T. S. Eliot and reprinted by permission of Harcourt, Brace and World, Inc.

Lewis Mumford, *The City in History* (New York, Harcourt, Brace and World, Inc., 1961), p. 117.

C. Wright Mills, "The Mass Society," *The Power Elite* (New York, Oxford University Press, 1959), pp. 320, 322.

Fred Cook and Gene Gleason, "The Shame of New York," *The Nation*, Vol. 189, No. 14, October, 1959, pp. 261–262. Copyright by *The Nation* and reprinted with its permission.

Lewis Mumford, *The City in History* (New York, Harcourt, Brace and World, Inc., 1961), p. 118.

Robert Nichols, "The City," *Dissent*, Vol. 8, No. 3, Summer 1961, pp. 219–221. Copyright 1961 by *Dissent* and reprinted with its permission.

George Bernard Shaw, "Too True to Be Good," *The Works of Bernard Shaw* (London, Constable and Company, Ltd., 1934), Vol. 31, p. 110.

Nathan Scott, *Modern Literature and the Religious Frontier* (New York, Harper and Brothers, 1958), pp. 92–93.

John Clellon Holmes, "The Philosophy of the Beat Generation," *The Beats* (New York, Faucett Publications, Inc., 1960), p. 22. Copyright 1958 by Esquire, Inc.

Marjorie Rittwagen, M.D., *The Sins of Their Fathers* (New York, Pyramid Books, 1959), p. 22.

Norman Mailer, "She Thought the Russians Was Coming," *Dissent*, Vol. 8, No. 3, Summer 1961, p. 412. Copyright 1961 by Dissent and reprinted by permission of the author.

Edgar Friedenberg, *The Vanishing Adolescent* (New York, Dell Publishing Co., 1959), pp. 193–194.

Albert Schweitzer, *Out of My Life and Thought* (New York, Holt, Rinehart and Winston, Inc., 1949), pp. 257–258.

D. H. Lawrence, *The Plumed Serpent* (New York, Knopf, 1951), pp. 73–74.

Alexis de Tocqueville, *Democracy in America*, translated by Henry Reeve (London, Oxford University Press, 1840), Part II, p. 488.

Keats, quoted in *America the Vincible* (New York, Doubleday and Co., 1959), p. 85.

Emmet John Hughes, *America the Vincible* (New York, Doubleday and Co., 1959), p. 86.

Langmead Casserly, *The Bent World* (New York, Oxford University Press, 1955), pp. 194–195.

Albert Camus, *Resistance, Rebellion, and Death*, translated by Justin O'Brien (New York, Alfred A. Knopf, 1961), p. 242. Reprinted with permission of the publishers.

Justice Learned Hand, *The Spirit of Liberty* (New York, Alfred A. Knopf, 1952), p. 190.

Reinhold Niebuhr, *Religion in America*, edited by John Cogley (New York, Meridian Books, Inc., 1958), p. 43.

Will Herberg, *Protestant, Catholic and Jew* (New York, Doubleday and Co., Inc., 1955), pp. 46–47.

Arthur Mann, "Charles Fleischer's Religion of Democracy," *Commentary*, Vol. 17, No. 6, June 1954, p. 557. Reprinted with permission of *Commentary* (copyright American Jewish Committee).

Jacques Maritain, *Reflections on America* (New York, Charles Scribner's Sons, 1958), pp. 186–187.

Robert McAfee Brown and Gustave Weigel, S.J., *An American Dialogue* (New York, Doubleday and Co., Inc., 1960), p. 30.

James Wechsler, *Reflections of an Angry Middle-Aged Editor* (New York, Random House, 1960), p. 16.

Daniel Bell, *The End of Ideology* (Glencoe, Ill., The Free Press, 1960), p. 288.

Reinhold Niebuhr, *The Children of Light and the Children of Darkness* (New York, Charles Scribner's Sons, 1944), pp. 16–17.

Gian-Carlo Menotti, *The Consul*, pp. 19–20, 41. Copyright 1950 by G. Schirmer, Inc., and reprinted by their permission.

Tom Driver, excerpt from drama review of *Look Back in Anger*, *The Christian Century*, Vol. 74, No. 43, October 23, 1957, p. 1263. Copyright 1957 by *The Christian Century* and reprinted with their permission.

Adam Margoshes, "The Fifth Column: My Religion," *The Village Voice Reader* (New York, Grove Press, 1963), pp. 262–263, copyright 1963 by The Village Voice, Inc., and used with their permission.

Jules Romaine, *Verdun: Men of Good Will* (New York, Alfred Knopf, Inc., 1939), p. 430.

Paul Elmen, *The Restoration of Meaning to Contemporary Life* (New York, Doubleday and Co., Inc., 1958), p. 48.

Dr. Gunther Anders, "The Phantom World of TV," *Mass Culture: The Popular Arts in America*, edited by Bernard Rosenberg and David M. White (Glencoe, Ill., The Free Press, 1957), pp. 358–367.

Eugene Ionesco, *Rhinoceros*, from *Rhinoceros and Other Plays*, translated by Derek Prouse (New York, Grove Press, Inc., 1960), p. 106. Copyright 1960 by John Calder. Reprinted by permission of Grove Press, Inc.

Peter Berger, *The Precarious Vision* (New York, Doubleday and Co., Inc., 1961), p. 65.

Arthur Sainer, from review of York Mystery Plays, *The Village Voice*, December 20, 1962. Copyright 1962 by The Village Voice, Inc., and reprinted by their permission.

DEDICATION

To Lorraine and the children who relinquished, partly, a husband and father for the sake of this book

I want to express my particular gratitude to a number of people without whose help and encouragement this would never have been finished: to Reverend Dean R. Wright and the Ministers and Missionary Board for providing a cloistered haven for writing; to Miss Shirley Cantrell, my secretary, who devoted time beyond the call of duty; to the congregation of Judson Church whose indulgence and understanding proffered me the time to write; and to numerous unnamed ones whose words and criticisms were invaluable in the completion of this book. A special thanks to Clara W. Mayer and the New School for Social Research who provided the lectureship upon which this book is based.

H. M.

Contents

Introduction

ONLY THE YOUNG or the foolish would undertake such a book, and it is devoutly to be wished that I classify as the former to be saved the shame of the latter. I cannot say in all honesty that I had a deep desire to put down my feelings, opinions and deep convictions about some of the problems that plague us in our time. The thought of it filled me with reservations, and the horror of writing a book and having to defend it the rest of my life left me with nothing but fear and trepidation. However, in a relatively short lifetime filled with uncautious undertakings, it has been a rule of thumb for me that I never refused a task simply because it was impossible. It has always seemed that the only criterion worth considering was—is it worth doing, and are you the one singled out for the task?

My philosophical, scientific and theological errors will be evident to all, but I do not apologize for these, for it is hoped that truth and error may cancel each other out so that we will be left with that poor, but most valuable substitute for supernatural clairvoyance or divine decree: namely, the limited, partial and finite knowledge of a single human being, a mixture of truth and falsehood, reason and feeling, intellect and viscera stamped with the singularity and uniqueness of one person's experience.

We are not the wisest persons who have dealt with the great problems and riddles which are the subject of this book and we may fail in our efforts to deal with them, but none of us can transfer the burden of our responsibility onto someone else's shoulder; we must think for ourselves and we must speak for ourselves and there is no substitute that modern education has conjured up for the honest, open wrestling of the human mind with the angel of truth until the daybreak of intellectual satisfaction finds us sore spent but happy that our curiosity and inquiry have been blessed.

I propose to speak my mind on these pages. If you find my conclusions erroneous, you will not be without consolation, for you can assure yourselves that I am totally mistaken; and there is that real possibility that I am. But there is hope that I may be enlightened. The words that follow are not ex cathedra doctrine but are meant to stimulate dialogue. No man living or dead can claim absolute authority or oracular power. My own view is a personal one, born of the experiences of my existence and bearing on it the marks of my own bias.

Now if you are like me and read many books, you may find yourself more interested in the writer than in what is written. And you may have questions and doubts about how he got where he is and whether or not his true feelings are revealed in what he is writing or whether he is wearing the costume of his party or profession. Thus we spend time shadowboxing rather than conversing with the one who writes. Perhaps then it would be helpful for me to speak directly to you about some of these personal biases.

First, I try not to take myself and what I have to say more seriously than I ought. This in no way indicates that I do not believe who I am or what I am saying is not significant, but when put in the context of the totality of things, I am able to detect the ludicrousness of any pompous claims to revelation. Man must always keep this perspective—it is called humor. The humor of a person or a culture is many times a more adequate index of spiritual depth than the religious perform- ances of overt piety. Even the Bible dares to speak of the laughter of God—and why not? What a spectacle it must be! It is the laughter that comes from watching *us*. We of the human race, who call ourselves "godlike," always claiming to philosophers, metaphysicians or men of wisdom. There never was a philosopher, whatever he said, no, nor man of science, whose conclusions ran counter to the dearest wishes of his heart, who worked against them, or condemned his hopes to death. There is real danger to all of our reason and logic when our deepest desires or self-interests are aroused.

One more disclaimer before I put forth the claims that will seem to deny all that I have written previously. There is no pretext to originality in the following pages. The ideas and words are the gift of others: teachers, friends, wise men who penetrated my mind with their thoughts. The uniqueness of what follows is the individual experience that collated the thoughts and meanings of others, impacted them with its own impression and offers them, humbly, as appropriated wisdom to cast light on the dark shadowy regions of our lives together.

Prolegomenon

NOW I WANT TO SAY a few words about this "world between the ages." Though as a descriptive phrase it may seem a little cryptic, part of its meaning is in the title—we are living in an "interim time" between the death of one age and prior to the beginning of a new one. I have already noted the grandiosity of the subject and the nature of my limitations in speaking of it, but now I would like to say a word about it.

Ortega y Gasset has a very helpful distinction in describing critical historical change. He says there are two kinds of such change: with one, something in the world changes, and with the other, the world itself changes. The crisis of our present era, I believe, is more like the latter. The world, the systems of belief which belonged to our forebears, has fallen away, and we remain without convictions. Due to the nature of this kind of radical historical change, this is always a very negative and critical period. There is a kind of disdain for all things which were once believed; everything that was nailed down as inevitable, inexorable, eternal, is coming loose, and the world itself somehow seems undependable. I rather believe that here I ought to turn to the world of poetry and myth to define what I mean, for they would probably yield more light than sociological analysis of the world between the ages. (This phrase has something of the apocalyptic about it, but it's more than that.) For it is the poets, the artists, the dramatists who have been the seismographic spirits of our age, recording the ominous rumblings beneath the thin veneer of our peace and affluence. William Butler Yeats describes our time in his poem "The Second Coming":

[xxi]

Turning and turning in the widening gyre
The falcon cannot hear the falconer;
Things fall apart; the centre cannot hold;
Mere anarchy is loosed upon the world,
The blood-dimmed tide is loosed, and everywhere
The ceremony of innocence is drowned;
The best lack all conviction, while the worst
Are full of passionate intensity.

"Things fall apart; the centre cannot hold"—this is characteristic of our world "between the ages." For example, the age of nationalistic provincialism and isolationism died on the battlefields of World War II, but the new age of universalism has not yet been born. We pretend we have shaken off the encumbrances of our racial and national tribalism, but, in spite of our sophistication, we are as frightened of the new age to come as an African primitive out of the hills shaking with fear and apprehension as he stands before the urban terrors of Johannesburg. In spite of all our talk we still act like the members of Ahab's crew in *Moby Dick* who were "nearly all Islanders," none "acknowledging the common continent of men but each *Isolato* living in a separate continent of his own."

To live "between the ages" means to live between the collapse of old orders and ways of living and the metanoia of a new kind of life, individually and collectively. It is a time of deep foreboding and even terror when our old gods have failed, when the answers, solutions and systems in which we trusted have proved impotent, and we live in the interim of unborn faiths, ideologies and ways of life. All the insecurities and uncertainties that accompany the sensation of shifting earth beneath our feet plague our existence. I remember the clairvoyant words of Josef Hromádka in *Doom and Resurrection* (published in 1945), when the author bespoke the ambiguity we have all since experienced:

"The feeling of restlessness, uncertainty, and divers suspicion as to the coming peace reveal our vague premonition that the very foundations of our future would have to be reshaped and rebuilt. Present humanity lives on some fragments and crumbs of the legally organized world."

It is true that we are living on the fragments of fractured faiths and eroded ethics which once guided and sustained our lives. So many "facts" and "absolute values" were stripped and exposed for what they were: social fictions and class biases by which we, individually and collectively, maintained our status and position. The solid ground of our social and theological presuppositions has shifted, and the proverbial sand threatens all our foundations.

In order to assess properly this world we keep talking about, we need to speak descriptively of some of its characteristics.

First, it is a world that has been passing through, not "the twilight zone" (that fantasy land would be welcome beside our own), but a zone of cosmic disturbances. From the Copernican revolution to the nuclear cataclysm, the structures of space in which men live have been turned awry, and we are feeling the resounding shock of psychological reverberations of man dislocated in space. How could we have known the paroxysm of passing from a finite world into an infinite one and the concussion to our psyches? A great scientist like Pascal in one of his *Fragments* expresses his fright in these words:

This is our true state and this is what makes us incapable of certain knowledge and of absolute ignorance. We sail within a vast sphere, ever drifting in uncertainty, driven from end to end. When we think to attach ourselves to any point and fasten to it, it wanders and leaves us, and if we follow it, it eludes our grasp, slips past us and vanishes forever. Nothing stays for us; this is our natural condition and yet most contrary to our inclination. We burn with desire to find solid ground and an ultimate sure foundation whereon to build a tower reaching to the infinite, but our whole groundwork cracks and the earth opens to abysses.

As it looks at the new universe, science finds no limit; and when psychologically we look into ourselves, we see no bottom.

This fathomless look makes for vertigo and even terror. If we are sensitive, we can see the effects of this dislocation and all of its spiritual aftermath upon man in New York, London, Leopoldville, Moscow and Hong Kong. In one place we find the detribalized primitive shorn of the unity of the tribe and the protection of its customs; we see him losing himself in a mine compound in South Africa or a shantytown in Elizabethville. Near him in misery we discover the displaced heir of a complex culture, torn from his origins, rootless and homeless, a refugee without a refuge. And then there is the "gray man" of many colors—the 1,500-calorie man for whom life is a struggle for bare existence. And at the other end of the range, we see modern intellectual man in search of something that will unite the myriad specializations that have disrupted knowledge and mislaid wisdom. And in between is the great mass of bewildered humanity made insecure and fearful by the breaking up of all they have known. W. H. Auden speaks for them in these words:

> What properties define our person since
> This massive vagueness moved in our lives
> What law requires our substance to exist
> Our strands of private order are dissolved
> And lost our routes to self-inheritance
> Position and relation are dismissed
> And epoch's Providence is quite worn out
> The lion of Nothing chases us about.

It is not only a world of cosmic disturbances, it is a world of war—this world between the ages, this world from Hiroshima to Berlin. It is a time when man has cried, "Peace! peace! and there is no peace." It is a world of wars of all kinds. There has been the *war of instruments,* actual war claiming lives and property, leaving its destruction and its scars upon the face of the earth. The trouble spots of the world are familiar names on the tongue of every schoolchild and are testimony to the breakdown of peace. The wars with instruments have been limited both in destruction and in geography, but they are ever-present preludes to unlimited and unimagined warfare which lies at our fingertips.

There has been a *war of nerves* spawned by the fears and apprehensions brought on by a great bipolar struggle for power and leadership and all our nuclear stockpiles prove the laws of diminishing returns. The psychological warfare takes its toll in mental disturbance and leads to breakdowns in many marginal people. It also leads to ludicrous, if not tragic, behavior patterns in which new housing subdivisions include bomb shelters with wall to wall carpeting (that helps with noise), color TV, and a year's supply of somebody's vermouth. Deserts and other unfit human habitations are being exploited and put up for sale on the basis that this location in "Happy Valley" will free one from the worries of the atomic age. The children of post-World War II are the inheritors of the influences of this age of the war of nerves.

Also, we are the daily spectators and victims of the *war of propaganda.* If the nerves are bombarded by fear, the mind is stretched taut and sometimes out of shape by the pull and strain of illogical logic and unreasonable reason. Everyday the hucksters of East and West play upon our minds with Orwellian confusion until war does become peace, and slavery does become freedom. Sorting out truth and falsehood, whether it be in the UN, in a political campaign, or in a newspaper editorial, becomes an impossible task before which we shrink and finally surrender; thus we become victims of the self-serving "truth" or withdraw from the whole world like a recluse.

This world between the times is a world where the old gods are dead and the new god is as yet unborn. It is a time when orthodox religions and traditional allegiances have been corroded away, and the foundation of all faiths has been shaken. In American culture where "faith" and "religion" have been such integral parts of our lives, it may be that we are slow to recognize the gradual disappearance of basic meta-physical presuppositions on which our lives and actions once firmly rested. Those who have come to recognize and admit that for them "God is dead" in the Nietzschean or Feuerbachian sense do not do so out of any arrogant defiance of God, but in a kind of tragic nostalgia for the God who has slipped from their lives. The outward show of religious resurgence—booming budgets, mounting memberships, and new buildings —will not serve to hide the impoverishment of all too much religious faith, nor to explain the paucity of our religion's influence upon the public life and morality of our nation.

All the characteristics of this world between the ages have an important influence upon postwar America. They become evident in every problem that faces our growing nation, and I want to focus on some of these in the following pages.

The
Fourth
Man

The Bourgeois Spirit

IT IS A thankless task and not always a very simple one to generalize about an era or a people, but it is important for us to see the safeguards we have put up against the "world between the ages," and the adjustments we Americans have made in order to cope with this new environment. One of the serious repercussions is the full-blown development of what I want to call the bourgeois spirit among the people of America. The following will be descriptive of the spirit of postwar America. If it appears to the reader to be irrelevant and incorrect, it will need to be ignored. On the other hand, if you recognize yourself as I have, you will be disturbed to realize what is happening to us.

I acknowledge the dangers and limitations in talking about the bourgeois spirit, because both words have been subject to a great amount of misuse and abuse. The word "bourgeois" will not be used in the sense of a Marxian epithet for "dirty, Wall Street capitalist," nor as a put-down of the avant-garde. Left to describe all those Philistine slobs who don't quote Rilke, nor listen to Stravinsky or see the hidden motif in Picasso's "Guernica." Also, it will not be used as a classification for the "middlebrow" of contemporary social researchers and cultural analysts. Rather it will be used as defined by the great Russian philosopher, Nikolai Berdyaev: "a spiritual state, a direction of the soul, a peculiar consciousness of being." He made it clear that the state of the bourgeois has existed in the world from the very beginning, and it has affected every social and economic class; its adherents have been both religious and nonreligious. For example, the man of means, distinction or achievement who is spiritually enslaved by that which he has gained or achieved and who enslaves others by that which he has won is a victim of the bourgeois spirit. But the poor man, the impoverished proletariat envying the rich man and spiritually enslaved by the desire to usurp his place and his wealth, is the same bourgeois. The active, frenetic go-getter of business, entertainment and profession, stepping on everyone, cutting and carving his way through people to the top of the ladder or his "place in the sun," is spiritually enslaved to the bourgeois spirit; but so are all the little shy and passive people at the bottom, looking up with adoration at the one who "made it." Seymour Krim puts it in vernacular in his essay on *Making It!*

Man, I know what I'm doing! I'm swinging instead of standing still, I'm racing with a racing age, I'm handling 17 things at once and I'm scoring with them all! Life's too wild today, sonny, to worry about the fate of the race or private morality or nun-like delicacies of should-I or should-I-not; anyone with brains or even imagination is a self-driven marauder with the wisdom to know that if he hustles hard enough he can have a moat full of gravy and a penthouse-castle high over life's East River! I'm bartering my neuroses for AT&T (not crying over them to Beethoven's Ninth like you, you fake holy man!) and bemoaning my futile existence with Mumm's Extra Dry and the finest hemp from Laredo and my new Jackson Pollock and my new off-Broadway boff and my new book and my new play and my new pad and this TV show they're gonna build around me and— Jesus, I've got it made!

. . . while down below the lusting average man and woman sweats in jealousy at the sight of these dexedrine angels, the very inspiration of what he and she can become if only they too can put that last shred of shame behind them and swing, extrovert yourself, get with it, make that buck, make that chick, make that poem, make this crazy modern scene pay off, O my heart, so I too can sink my teeth in the sirloin and wear the pearls of hell!

The bourgeois spirit cuts across all the categories we concoct for putting people in their places. It is found not only in

America (to the chagrin of a large number of Europhiles), but may be detected in London, Paris, Berlin, Johannesburg, Moscow and Hong Kong. There are recognizable marks of the bourgeois spirit wherever its victims are and whatever condition they are in.

First, the bourgeois is completely bound to this world without any reference to the transcendent, which is a level of being, of spirit that is the same order as grace, mercy, and love. This *"concupiscence of the temporal,"* into which we fall before we are aware of it, denies the claim that makes us essentially human; namely that we do not belong entirely to that world of objects and things into which men are seeking to absorb us, in which they are trying to confine us. The bourgeois, in a theological sense of that word, is the person who can believe only in the visible world—he does not know that he suffers from a blindness which prevents him from seeing, in depth, so many visible things in this world, let alone the invisible. The bourgeois desires to occupy a position of strength and power, to establish himself firmly, and to arrange the laws and the order of this world so that it secures his position. The bourgeois spirit is unemancipated and subjects a man's whole life to external determination, making him look like a poor vassal whose loud bravadoes about freedom cannot cover the pity of his imprisoned life.

There is an unforgettable passage in Antoine de Saint-Exupéry's *Wind, Sand and Stars*. In a ride to the airport with some government officials, one character muses:

Old bureaucrat, my comrade, it is not you who are to blame. No one ever helped you to escape. . . . You rolled yourself up into a ball in your genteel security, in routine, in the stifling conventions of provincial life, raising a modest rampart against the winds and the tides and the stars. You have chosen not to be perturbed by great problems having trouble enough to forget your own fate as man. You are not the dweller upon an errant planet and do not ask yourself questions to which there are no answers. You are a petty bourgeois of Toulouse. Nobody grasped you by the shoulder while there was still time. Now the clay of which you were shaped has dried and hardened, and naught in you will ever awaken the sleeping musician, the poet, the astronomer that possibly inhabited you in the beginning.

This is the fate of the true bourgeois steeped in the "orderly jungles of his own profound abstractions"; he explains everything about life except what it means to be human.

The bourgeois *lives in awe and captivity of the technical and the mechanical.* His technological activity, which he embraces as part of his deliverance—seeking what is better (whether mousetrap or Thor rocket), expanding his power, pushing back the limits of his world past all measurements— becomes a frightening development.

He has helped to create a whole bourgeois scientific tradition which claims a "realism" toward life that is as much an anomaly as anything else. The material reality on which the bourgeois man places his whole realism is only part of total reality. The freedom of dreams, the illogicality of the subconscious, the inexplicable terror of the demonic, the awareness of the absurd in life are also part of the ultimate truth of being. So that to accept only the scientific and technical facts about man is to degrade his dignity and reduce him to a robot. It is this mark of the bourgeois that transcends all differences and reveals the fundamental similarity of the bourgeois whether living in Russia or in America. The ferocity of commitment to this narrow dimension of life reveals an incomplete conception of reality that is falsified and mechanized.

The dramatist Ionesco saw with great clarity this trait in modern man and writes these perceptive words in a critical essay, *La Démystification pa l'humour noir (L'avant-Scene, 15,* February, 1955):

. . . the Stalinist bourgeoisie whether in Russia or in the West being devoid of understanding has forbidden the imagination to be imaginative, that is to be free and in the exercise of its freedom to be a revealer of truth; realism rears its ugly head, a narrow brand of *realism,* confined to a single plane of truth so narrow, so distorted by its own fanaticism, that it turns out, in the end, to be a plane of total unreality. . . .

To live in captivity to a scientific realism that is truly unreality is part of what cuts off the bourgeois man from so much of life. This is part of the reason the bourgeois has little grasp of the past and has lost his sense of history—either personal or collective. Every individual is historically unique, created out of a mysterious past which controls him—a past formed of oral tradition, the influence of family and friends, customs and habits and some kind of common faith. In technological society, however, the individual can be comprehended and made, planned for down to the last detail of his annuity and pension, transposed at will and identically duplicated—and all of this without conscious past. The individual is only a means, a part or a function—and he can be replaced like the worn-out machine he has grown to resemble. In Virgil Gheorgious' *The 25th Hour* a character named Trajan says:

In the most recent phase of its development Western civilization is no longer taking account of the individual and there seems to be no ground for hoping that it will ever do so again. That society knows only a few of the dimensions of the individual; man in his wholeness considered as an individual no longer exists for it. The West has created a society which resembles a machine. It forces men to live and adapt themselves to the laws of the machine. When men come to resemble machines sufficiently to identify themselves with machines, then there will be no more men on the face of the earth.

Man no longer lives by the unconquerable hopes of his race— he is satisfied with the superficial of everyday. The eternal mysteries of life, the illimitable riddles of our universe no longer puzzle or attract him. Heaven is here in every parking place we find; the secrets of the universe are encompassed in the latest electronic gadget, and peace is our profit. Most of us have died immersed in the mechanical life, fully ignorant of the magnitude of our existence. The bourgeois spirit suffers a loss of the feeling for living, and such an enslavement by technical mastery can only end in despair. We are the prisoners of a progress which is at once false and deceptive. Every advance in technique seems to us an inevitable step forward, and so we are caught in the cause-and-effect fatality of modern mechanical determinism. What we seem to want is a bad angel to do the dirty work and a good angel to take care of the nobility while we give ourselves up to the slavish routine of a propagandized fate.

Another mark of the bourgeois spirit is *the love of things and a possessiveness about things.* The affluence of our present society accentuates this factor considerably, and it is an honest reflection upon what happens to life—my own and yours—in the best of all possible worlds. We might as well face it—we eat better, travel faster, live more comfortably, enjoy more cushions and crutches than any generation in any country in any time. This ought not be just the patriotic boast of slick paper ads, but a sobering thought, and one which ought to give us pause. Does our affluence blind us to the problem we still have? Have we not been lulled by our condition so that we think all the answers are at least close at hand, and that a welfare state run by practical and intelligent men (preferably from Harvard) will save us from disasters and catastrophes of all kinds? Isn't there something a little unreal about our euphoria, something a little smug about our self-confidence? Ambrose Bierce once defined optimism as "the doctrine or belief that everything is beautiful including what is ugly." Some of our cultural critics are suggesting that perhaps we haven't faced what our plenty really means and how it has shaped and misshaped our character as a people. One of them, Thomas Griffith, says that when we talk about our pursuit of false values we really are giving ourselves too much credit.

Rather it is that progress has us in its tow and is dragging us so fast we don't know how to let go, for progress moves with momentum not its own, and sets such a fast pace that we don't know how to let go. It's all very exciting, but, as this critic soberly warns us, "despite the multiplicity of advantages and advances it sometimes seems a bleak windswept tarmac, we occupy, on the airstrip of the future."

Here is the warning and it comes from many sources, some unexpected: despite all the benumbing fear that we will blow ourselves to hell, the chances are greater that we shall perish not of incineration but of "soul rot." No matter how "good we've got it," there is an imperative lying heavily on our shoulders to examine our collective lives in the light of this danger. There cannot be in the life of nations any more than in our personal lives a period of rest when we do not have to struggle with fundamental problems. How callous has our comfort made us? I think we are growing more insensitive to the pockets of persistent poverty in our own country and the unimaginable inequities between America and the rest of the world.

We have always made a great deal of the pursuit of happiness in our country to the neglect of many other kinds of meaningful pursuits, and that pursuit seems always to be marked as a pursuit after more goods and economic advantage. Walter Reuther speaks of America becoming a circus civilization devoting itself to "communal happiness hunts." But the important question is whether or not the better off we are, the fuller we feel, the thicker our hides grow and the dimmer our vision, the more we lose the capacity to hear and identify with the desperate cries of need of those suffering in hunger, deprivation and oppression just around the corner from our prosperity.

Recently in a survey of Manhattan, it was found that 49.3 percent of nonwhite families had a median income of less

than $3,999. Nearly 317,000 families in the city had a total
family income of less than $3,000. And in the rest of the
nation things look no better. In a 1962 Report of the Confer-
ence on Economic Progress, entitled *Poverty and Deprivation
in the United States,* we are told that seventy-seven million
Americans live in poverty and deprivation. In view of the
unparalleled rate of improvement in living standards and the
amazing growth of affluence since the 1930's, it is a far greater
indictment than the much larger number that lived that way
three decades ago.

We have been reminded in recent months of that uncom-
fortable paradox of contemporary history: that as America has
become richer, much of the world has become increasingly
poorer. One report out of the United Nations tells us that
the underfed of this world standing side by side would stretch
around the globe twenty-five times. As populations explode,
the circle is expanding twenty miles a day. I know these are
only numbers, but as Bishop Gore reminded us, "true charity
is the ability to read statistics with compassion." The poverty
that plenty brings us may be measured in the distance that it
puts between us and the dispossessed of our own country and
the rest of the world. Now I know you may say these are
serious technical and economic problems that we should leave
to economists, but I believe that is a latter-day dodge calculated to unload our responsibility. Berdyaev once said that
"Bread for myself is an economic problem; bread for my
brother is a spiritual one." We may have solved one problem,
but the other is begging for our attention.

What happens to the moral judgments and ethical decisions, to the soul and spirit of a people so saturated by a thing-
centered culture? It seems sometimes that what really plagues
us in our affluence is not that the Bureau of Internal Revenue
will require an accounting, but that Someone will require our
soul—and ask us what has happened to the life of the spirit.

I am as convinced as the next person that some of the vast inequalities of the 1920's and 1930's have been corrected (and I am happy for it), but, for example, I am appalled at the lack of indignation, at the life of luxury we lead in a city like New York, while we force our children to go to school in lousy, crummy fire traps; that we can build a fabulous Lincoln Center for the Performing Arts and leave thousands of people performing life in deplorable, rat-infested tenements; that we indulge city officialdom in the Cadillac society at the same time we keep sick and injured people waiting outside dilapidated and ill-manned city hospitals. We are an immensely wealthy nation comprising only 6 percent of the population living in an impoverished world. Yet, we are afraid that "handouts" and "giveaways" might ruin our economy; and lawmakers, promoting the idea of foreign aid, must dress it up as prudent self-interest before they can sell it to the people. All of this is the mark of a people immersed in a world of things, saturated with plenty, yet displaying a disproportionate concern for security and at times a psychotic anxiety about all that we *have* and are.

Now it seems that this love of things and the affluence which we have enjoyed have left two indelible impressions on our individual lives and on our national character: *the loss of courage and commitment and the fear of death.*

First, I want to deal with the lack of courage and commitment. It might be helpful to describe what I believe is the psychological-spiritual mood of our people in this "world between the ages," for this provides the context of our "failure of nerve." A profound indifference and apathy are abroad in the land. Amid our bewilderment, we seek a haven that will be as comfortable and secure as possible. That haven may be an East Side penthouse, a hideaway in exurbia, a pad in Greenwich Village or just a cozy, insulated mind-set, but principally we find it in withdrawal and resignation, and a

refusal to commit ourselves wholeheartedly to anything except this indifference.

We are unwilling or loath to give our all *de profundis* to
anyone—not the party, not reform, not even to peace. We
may join a cause or causes and work hard in them, but we
still hold back in our inner recesses and have not genuinely
given ourselves—nay, seem incapable of doing so. Real convictions and commitment are a novelty at which people smile
wistfully, except the conviction that we can make no real commitments. We are not interested in involvement and adventure;
we hate risks and gambles, and these are all we find. We don't
want to get too emotionally involved with anything—not our
job, not our lover and not even our psychiatrist. We do not
want to subject ourselves to hurt or leave ourselves vulnerable.
Having reached out our hands only to have them burned by
disappointment and disillusion, we are conditioned by life
itself to keep our hands in territory that is relatively safe.
We yearn to be detached, neutral spectators, though we would
like to be enlightened spectators, sophisticated in our consumption of journalism. None are so prone to this temptation
as those who deem themselves to be intellectual. Franz Werfel
uses the figure of the theater to describe us:

There is no fiercer pride in the world than that of the intellectual.
Though hungry and shelterless he is sure that God did not place
him on life's stage but invited him to sit in the royal box. The
"consciousness that he does not belong to mimes who play the
play but among the objective observers fills him with the intoxica-
tion of superiority which makes even the life of want endurable."

We see ourselves not as actors in the drama of life, but
spectators. Our task, we think, is judging whether the drama
is entertaining or boring, tragic or comic, has a good plot or
no plot.

We are in bondage to anxiety, hostility and guilt. We find
it difficult to point to what we fear; we fear fear itself. We
cannot always localize our hostility, but we are hostile toward

almost everyone and everything; we do not feel guilty about anything in particular, we just feel guilty. We have the feeling of a powerful, inescapable danger against which we are helpless and impotent. Hence, we are anxious in our blind striking out at the unknown foe. We are hostile that we should be dealt such a fate; we are guilty that we are helpless, for we love to think of ourselves as independent, autonomous, rational beings who can control any situation. We try to escape this battle of attrition in many ways: by joining every status organization we can to gain recognition; by burying ourselves in books and attempting to become an intellectual; by joining the rat race as an enlightened despot in the ruthless, competitive struggle; by becoming a pious priest, condemning the transgressions of all sinners; by becoming a self-abnegating hair shirt, chastising the affluent profligates of the land. There is nothing we will not, cannot and do not use as an escape from our hostility, anxiety and guilt, and as a prop for our own security.

I would submit that the loss of courage is a concomitant of the spiritual condition we have been describing. Only a people who have greatly oversimplified life and cut down the magnitude of existence until it fits in the pockets of their understanding would dare to relegate courage to such a place of insignificance in the catalog of human virtue. To face the normal experiences of living is to exhibit courage. Dr. Kurt Goldstein says that "courage in its final analysis is nothing but an affirmative answer to the shocks of existence which must be borne that one's own nature may be actualized." In other words, it takes courage just to be oneself. In Paul Tillich's exhaustive examination of *The Courage to Be,* he says that courage is the essential self-affirmation of one's being and that "the 'courage to be' is an ethical act in which man affirms his own being in spite of those elements of his existence which conflict with his self-affirmation."

Now let it be clear that the courage we are talking about

is not the courage of despair, of which contemporary literature is full to brimming, for here man is essentially bitter and despairing; he is immersed in despair—to live is to cry out continually in cosmic anxiety that all is doom and we are the recipients of Nothing. Because of this we are bitter and angry. Like Caitlin Thomas, Dylan's widow, who says in her autobiographical *Leftover Life to Kill,* "My bitterness is not an abstract substance; it is solid as a Christmas cake. I can cut it in slices and hand it around and there is plenty left for tomorrow." In other words, contemporary literature characterizes all of us as disaster-bound humans, not tragic but pathetic, wallowing in self-pity, helpless to use our own freedom and utterly imprisoned by our drives and passions, which have shut themselves off from the rest of humanity. No, we've seen enough serious-minded youth sitting in nonalcoholic coffeehouses, getting drunk with existential despair!

Rather we are talking about the courage of confidence that enables us to act, to make decisions, to rise or fall upon our convictions, the kind of courage required to face the inward growth of the self and all that it involves of separation and loneliness and frustration. Perhaps much of the retarded adolescence of our time and the inability to grow up to become independent selves are due in no small measure to a "failure of nerve," a lack of courage to pay the price of new levels of freedom. And this involves the courage not just to be oneself but to give oneself for the sake of another. I think Balzac's description of this kind of courage comes closest to what we are speaking about:

The quality that above all deserves the greatest glory in art—and by that word we must include all creations of the mind—is courage, courage of a kind which common minds have no conception . . . to plan, dream, and imagine fine works is a pleasant occupation to be sure. But to produce, to bring to birth, to bring up the infant work with labor, to put it to bed full fed with milk, to take up again every morning with inexhaustible, matured love, to lick it

clean, to dress it a hundred times in lovely garments that it tears
up again and again, never to be discouraged by the convulsions of
this mad life, and to make a living masterpiece that speaks to all
eyes in sculpture, or to all minds in literature, to all memories in
painting, to all hearts in music—that is the task of execution. . . .
If the artist does not throw himself into his work like a soldier
into the breach and if, in that crater he does not dig like a miner
buried under a fall of rock, the work will never be completed.

This is the kind of courage required in this mass, collectivis-
tic society every time a person moves one step toward being
an individual in his own right, for all our institutions and
organizations have a way of smothering or stamping out the
off-trail, creative, refractory, stubborn impulses to selfhood
and an individualized vision of things. I fear for us that we may
have lost the most precious liberty of all—*the freedom and
courage to risk one's life for anything or anyone,* and by "one's
life" I mean every security and status and possession as well
as breath and blood. We are like Jean Baptiste Clamence, in
Camus' *The Fall,* paralyzed by the voice of the drowning
woman in the night, unable to move a muscle to save her, but
subsequently longing to hear that voice again that he might
redeem his guilt-ridden, cowardly soul. Some time ago, in a
CBS report on the Berlin situation and its present status, one
of the commentators from England said these words, "There
is not a single person in all of England willing to die over
West Berlin," and this seems to me an ominous note. I don't
believe for a moment that the Berlin situation is a single one,
nor am I in the least sympathetic to those who think that a
warlike move in that critical spot will show the Russians we
mean business, but the illuminating part of that statement is
what seems to lie behind it, namely, that there is nothing we
can bring ourselves to die for, either in England or America.
I appreciate the indignant humanitarianism behind the words,
"I would rather be Red than dead," but they reveal far more
than a protest against the horror of nuclear holocaust. They

bespeak of an idolatry of life, so enslaved by what we are and *have* that we will not risk death. Does all of our condemnation and petitioning and banner-waving about the genocide of nuclear war really grow out of our deep-seated humanity, or does it perhaps reveal, more than we care to admit, a gnawing doubt in our hearts that there is anything or anyone *worth* dying for, let alone destroying the world for. Or at least, if there is, we lack the courage to give ourselves, to risk the price of involvement which could mean losing all we *have*.

This then takes us to the next step—the bourgeois spirit and the attitude toward death. I am sure that the *fear of death* (this is not to judge against a universal wish for it) is deeply involved in the loss of courage and the unwillingness to commit ourselves to anything. Not our emancipation from the superstitions of hell and heaven nor our sophisticated stoicism about life, nor our daily anticipation of universal destruction adds any dimension to our ability to face death. Every one of us knows the obsessional insanity of the fear of death which covers us at times like a heavy cloud, shutting out the light and cutting us off from the presence of anyone else.

Now our way of meeting death is camouflage; pretend that it is not there—throw a sheet over the whole business. Our methods of the evasion of death are just as systematized and depersonalized as our ways of escaping life. The Rest Havens and Forest Lawns, the mortuary chapel with its soft hush and rose-colored drapes, the deep banks of flowers and artificial grass to cover the good black earth—these are all part of the escape. All that music, perfume, science and hygiene can do is used to create an evasive womblike world of comfort and soft sympathy. Death is thus brought within the orbit of a consumer world and is neutralized by an absorption into irrelevant patterns of thought, feeling and techniques. So in the final analysis, death gets the same treatment as sex in our modern world—made a part of a fantasy-like dream world where it is depersonalized and depassioned.

However, all our attempts to cover up or ignore death will not hide the deep-seated fears each of us entertains of seeing our own obituary. But those of us who are prisoners of our progress and inheritors of affluence have a better chance of pulling off the evasion of death than others in our culture. William Stringfellow, a young lawyer friend of mine who practices in East Harlem amidst the squalor, depression and poverty of that vast neighborhood, wrote recently in *The Christian Century* about his experiences there: "What sophisticates the suffering of the poor is not any innocence nor its extremity, nor its loneliness nor the fact that it is unknown or ignored by others, but rather the lucidity, the straightforwardness with which it bespeaks the power and presence of death among men in this world. The awful and ubiquitous claim of death is not different for the poor than for other men or for that matter for nations and ideologies or other principalities or powers, but among the poor there are no grounds to rationalize the claim, no way to conceal it, no facile refutation of the claim, no place to be securely hidden from the claim."

The insulation of wealth, the social fictions, the institutional facades protect us from the facing of death.

Now in all that I have been saying about the bourgeois spirit and the effects of affluence on the character of the American people, I am fully aware of the dangers of generalization, and one can think of those exceptions that make untrue the foregoing conclusions about us. Therefore I want to address myself to the exceptions in our culture—those persons or groups which do not conform to the picture I have been painting of the predominant "geist" of our time. I want to note with some interest that these exceptions are manifestly antisocial or illegal by nature: they are the street-corner society or gang

subcultures of the large cities of this country, and the Freedom Riders. While I do not hold up these groups as models,
I do insist that they produce a certain morality and ethical
discipline that shames much of our respectable bourgeois
culture.

The street-corner society, for example, spawns a strange
breed of human beings who do not share our mores and morals
and, as a matter of fact, behave like "the young savages" we
picture them to be. We do not really understand them because
we always see them (from a distance) through the eyes of a
social worker, a psychiatrist, a policeman, or a teacher, some
authority figure who shares the same values and abhors the
same uncouthness we do. We need to know them, to listen to
their speech for those words that are the index to their inner
turmoil, and for those inflections of language that belie the
deep desire of their hungry spirits for something they can
give themselves to. Their sexual bravadoes and recounting of
"kicks" cover an abyss of emptiness.

Nevertheless, their lives together in the gang produce a
kind of morality that causes its members to risk their lives
for each other and for their gang, and over matters which you
and I would consider unworthy. Again, my lawyer friend from
East Harlem says that these adolescents court danger for
strange objectives, "like jurisdiction over a street that is filled
with garbage or a girl who probably is not a virgin," and I
don't think we can begin to understand this "waste of life"
as we call it. It is the opposite from us who wouldn't think
of actually giving up our life for another, much less for what
seems of so little worth. But these kids of the streets have
developed that freedom about which we spoke earlier: the
freedom to give their lives for the sake of another, even if that
person or thing seems altogether undeserving. What is the
relation between the fact that "not one Englishman is willing
to die over Berlin" and any number of Sportsmen (a "bopping"

gang) are willing to die over only a block of a crummy lower
East Side street? The question ought not to be answered
quickly or glibly, nor especially with some moralistic exhorta-
tions about juvenile delinquents.

Another exception in our American cultural scene to the
general prevalence of the bourgeois spirit is the phenomenon
of the young Negro leadership of the South that gave direction
and impetus to the Freedom Rides, the sit-ins, the pray-ins
and all other forms of cutting short the long day's journey
toward human dignity and rights. Out of the mediocrity and
the moderation of the fifties came this strange mutation of
persevering courage and impatient action, marking the rise
of a new generation (albeit sectional and a minority) that
seems to give lie to so much of the analysis we have been
making.

Here were people who found in these apathetic and timid
times the "courage to be" and an aptitude for living non-
chalantly (with songs and prayers on their lips) in the face of
danger and the threat of death. Many gave up the relative
security of that unendurable status quo of hat-tipping submission and smothered dissent that the white South has offered
them for so long. These young people sacrificed family peace,
their education and their liberty for a chance to say that which
came out of the depths, not of their own suffering, for they
were young, but of their parents' long years of shame and
humiliation as second-class persons. In the face of the rise of
these young people to claim their legacy, there was equal in-
credulity in the eyes of the Negro parents and the white people
of this country. Neither seemed to be able to understand this
new breed of protestants that stood up to be counted, marked
and imprisoned in a time when everybody was sitting down,
hoping to be overlooked. How to explain these strange deviants
in our culture who with their fervent voices in song and speech
put an end to all our chidings of "silent generation" and our

caricature of the younger generation as one with "frozen feet and leaden hearts"? If we could not explain them, at least we could be grateful that they came into our history at such a time, bucking the tide of conformity, apathy and middle-of-the-roadism and planting in our midst living examples of audaciousness and human valor.

Now what about these exceptions and contradictions to the bourgeois spirit? Do they make untenable our stand regarding the dominant spirit of our times? It would seem so, but there is one significant common denominator in these glaring exceptions to this influence of the bourgeois spirit—namely, without exception these groups generally have not had access to the affluence and prosperity which seem to have secluded us from our "pain-fellows" in this world. These groups are without the economic advantages and social status that make conformists of us all. None of them have had the luxury of any secure hiding place from deprivation, suffering or the intimidation of death in this life; none of them were prevented by wealth or position from enduring the bruises and struggles of life's buffeting; all of the members of these groups stood impotent before the socially strong, legally-oriented and politically powerful allies of society. For example, how often in the past few years have we heard the courageous acts of the Freedom Riders and sit-ins condemned on the grounds that they were a threat to the very basis of law and order?

It appears, then, that the deepest resistance to the prevailing mood of the bourgeois spirit, incarnated in acts of courage and costly commitment, is most dramatically portrayed in those persons born on the other side of the tracks from life's privileges and plenty. At least it is they who have given us the hope that resistance is possible once we know and admit the true nature of our enslavement.

The Exploration of Inner Space

IN A WORLD of psychological dislocations, where "the center cannot hold" and Freud opened up a veritable Pandora's box of egos and ids, it was natural that men, rather than face inward, would turn outward to the world, concentrating on practical matters of progress and looking for new worlds more secure than the one opening up to them.

Without sounding like some Cassandra, I want to register my grave misgivings about the dangerous direction and imbalance of our progress, both scientific and social. Progress seems to be forever outrunning both our ability to cope with it and the failure to assimilate properly the *last* step in our forward movement. When I began to think about the matter, my mind turned to the frontiers of new spaces we have faced as Americans and the part that they have played in our lives and the influences they have had on the cultic practices and social ideology of our country. I want to mention only briefly three of those frontiers where search and research have challenged our lives as Americans.

First, there is the *horizontal* one. This is geographical and physical by nature—the pushing back of the rugged frontiers that served as the physical borderlands of civilization. With physical stamina, willpower and fortitude, men pushed back the geographical wilderness until it gave up to them cultivated land, towns, and new kinds of existence. The invasion and conquering of this frontier have been celebrated in song and story, and they produced the frontiersmen, heroes like Daniel

[19]

Boone, Lewis and Clark, James Bowie and countless others known and unnamed. From one end of this nation to the other, the land was explored, tracked and mapped. People huddled together in patches of sociability called villages, and roads and paths interlaced the wildernesses and countrysides, joining farms and towns.

When Americans had pushed back the last vestiges of the forest primeval, tracked every brook and river to the sea, named the valleys, the hills and the mountains, they stood like restless, dissatisfied creatures, looking for their next frontier. In some parts of the world the horizontal thrust goes on; new spaces and regions are being explored and opened up to settlement and civilization. But in this country, except for an occasional brave soul who defies the uncharted regions of some wild lake or mountain country, our geographical frontier has been pushed to the limit.

Then there is another frontier, the *vertical* one rather than the geographical. This is cultural and material—the onward and upward thrust seen in architecture, careers, finances and production. When the last frontier of geography passed from their grasp, Americans reached for this new one. There was no place to go from the earth but up—so buildings shot skyward along with everything else. In the world of business and commerce, the ladder of success was set clearly before everyone to climb. Henry Clews, a noted banker at the turn of the century, gave this advice to Yale students in 1908:

You may start in business or professions with your feet on the bottom rung of the ladder; it rests with you to acquire the strength to climb to the top. You can do so if you have the will and thrusts to do so. There is always plenty of room at the top. . . . Success comes to the man who tries to compel success to yield to him. Cassius spoke well to Brutus when he said, 'The fault is not in our stars, dear Brutus, that we are underlings, but in our natures.'

It followed as night the day that men who had pushed back the wilderness frontiers would not be content to sit back and allow the new frontier to go unexplored and unconquered. The heroes of this new frontier were the Jim Fisks, the Andrew Mellons, and the John D. Rockefellers. It might be noted here that President Kennedy's "new frontier" of campaign oratory, if not of actual performance, was this vertical one in its most naked form. It was spoken to Americans who long nostalgically for the time when there were new worlds to conquer, new foes to overcome, new and difficult heights to climb.

Now the third frontier is neither horizontal nor vertical exactly but rather *curved*, for it is the outward one—the new space of outer atmosphere, stratosphere and ionosphere. Outer space has been in the minds of scientists and fiction writers for years, but it dawned on the consciousness of most Americans with the advent of Sputnik I. We were catapulted into the space age when we began one of the largest and most concentrated scientific research tasks in the history of any people. The challenge to our minds and our practical ingenuity filled the gap left by the disappearance of other frontiers. But if this new frontier had its thrilling aspects, it also had its dark side. *Tomorrow Is Already Here,* Robert Jungk's travelogue of terror through the technological jungle of our own "brave new world" of Univacs, rockets and missiles, must give us some pause. He tells of how men are shaken, beaten, scalded, kneaded, frozen, suffocated and crushed. It is happening daily to dozens of young Americans preparing for outer space. All of this is happening because we have set out on our longest journey to an unknown destination, and the journey leads to places only God has named and where men were probably never intended to go and for which he as an organism has not been fitted by nature.

There is one story about an Air Force instructor at Randolph Field in Texas who formulated this outlook in the following categorical assertion: "Measured by the flying task that lies ahead of him, man is a faulty construction." And eighty cadets listening to the lecture noted this simplification in

their shorthand notes: "Man . . . is a faulty construction."
As frail human beings, we seem to be unfitted for this race
in every way, but we are determined to make it. Undoubtedly,
we will solve all the physical problems that make man a
"faulty construction" for the limits of outer space. His flesh
will be made endurable; his breathing will be simulated; and
there is already a pill which eliminates all waste from a man's
body while in space flight. But what about man's mind?
There is the nub of the problem and experiment goes on apace.
Listen to this quote from a scientific paper, "Space Cabin
Requirements as Seen by Subject in the Cabin Simulator," by
Dr. Willard Hawkins, USAF School of Aviation Medicine:

Time began to weigh heavily for the subject early in the flight, and
as time went on it seems that the oppressiveness of time increased
in a ratio directly proportional to the duration of the flight. Inter-
mittent periods of depression similar to depressive moods which
result from extreme monotony have been routinely observed in
all subjects at sometime during their flight . . . The clicking noise
of the camera shutter that automatically took a picture of the subject every three minutes during the flight became a major source
of irritation for one subject after ninety-two hours in the cabin.
All the subjects enjoyed music during the work period but soon
found that their favorite recordings were highly irritating as they
were repeated.

How like the human species—always unfitted for what is
before him—unfit to live together on the face of the earth and
unfit to seek the refuge of outer space. It is as Rilke lamented
in his "Diurno Elegie":

Each sluggish turn of the world has such disinherited,
To whom belongs neither what's been nor what's coming next.

However, it looks as though there is no checking the fever
now that we have the regions of outer space to explore, lay
our claim to and conquer. There is little time in this madden-
ing world of the race for space to put any questions to ourselves about the premium we have put on the capture and

consolidation of this new outer frontier. There seems little chance that these questions will penetrate the pillbox and pad world of calculators, chronometers and countdowns.

The point being raised here is not that history should go backward or science be repudiated or space research be cut out but, as Bergson so profoundly warned us, that every kind of development of outward techniques ought to be balanced in man by an effort at inner conquest. It seems an obvious truth that in our contemporary world the more we become dependent on gadgets and techniques the more alienated we seem to become from the awareness of our inner reality.

At least we ought to probe the wisdom of our reactions to Sputnik I when we grabbed every gifted child we could find and shoved him into science and math to close the gap between Russia and us. It was founded on the premise that nothing but good can come if we win the race to outer space and establish our beachheads on the edge of the stars before anyone else. I want to quote from two sources that raise thoughtful questions about man as unriddler and ruler of outer space. The first is from the novelist C. S. Lewis in his book, *Perelandra*. Describing one of his characters, he says:

Professor Weston . . . was a man obsessed with the idea which is at this moment circulating all over our planet in obscene works of "scientifiction" in little Interplanetary Societies and Rocketry clubs . . . ignored or mocked by the intellectuals but ready, if ever the power is put into its hands, to open a new chapter of misery for the universe. It is the idea that humanity, having now sufficiently corrupted the planet where it arose must at all cost contrive to seed itself over a larger area . . . beyond this lies the sweet poison of the false infinite—the wild dream that planet after planet, system after system, in the end galaxy after galaxy can be forced to sustain everywhere and forever the sort of life contained in the loin of our species—a dream begotten by the hatred of death upon the fear of true immortality.

And the second source is a broadcast several years ago by Eric Sevareid, part of which I think bears repeating here:

. . . the lovely and luminous moon has become a public issue. For quite a few thousand years it was a private issue; it figured in purely bilateral negotiations between lovers, in the incantations of jungle witch doctors and Indian corn planters. Poets from attic windows issued the statements about the moon. The moon was always measured in terms of hope and reassurance and the heart pangs of youth . . . it is now measured in terms of mileage and foot-pounds of rocket thrust. Children sent sharp sweet wishes to the moon, now they dream of blunt-nose missiles.

There must come a time, in every generation, when those who are older secretly get off the train of progress, willing to walk back where they came from, if they can find the way. We're afraid we're getting off now. Cheer if you wish the first general or Ph.D. who splatters something on the kindly face of the moon. We shall grieve for him and for ourself, for the young lovers and poets and dreamers to come because the ancient moon will never be the same again. Therefore, we suspect the heart of man will never be the same.

We find it very easy to wait for the first photographs of the other side of the moon for we have not yet seen the other side of Lake Louise or the Blue Ridge peak that shows through the cabin window. We find ourself quite undisturbed by the front-page talk of "controlling the earth from the moon" because we do not believe it. If neither men nor gadgets can control the earth from the earth, we fail to see how they will do so from the moon.

It is exciting talk indeed, the talk of man's advance toward space. But one little step in man's advance toward man—that, we think would be truly exciting. Let those who wish try to discover the composition of a lunar crater. We would settle for discovering the true mind of a Russian commissar or the inner heart of a delinquent child. There is, after all, another side—a dark side to the human spirit, too. Men have hardly begun to explore these regions and it is going to be a very great pity if we advance upon the bright side of the moon with the dark side of ourselves, if the cargo in the first rockets to reach there consists of fear, and chauvinism and suspicion. Surely we ought to have our credentials in order, our hands very clean and perhaps a prayer for forgiveness on our lips as we prepare to open the ancient vault of the shining moon.

This is not a plea to turn back the wheels of time in man's quest for new frontiers or even halt his scientific march to wherever, but I do want to suggest that a balance is necessary, and that there is another frontier that modern man has overlooked and neglected in his preoccupation with the horizontal, vertical and curved frontiers.

This is the inner frontier of man's life—*inner space*. By nature this new area of inner exploration is not geographical or physical but personal, artistic, lyrical and psychological. Now this has been here all along, but we have left its exploration to mystics and contemplatives. I would submit to you that at least part of the crisis of our time is due to the neglect of this frontier—its identification and exploration. There probably are good reasons why man has been blocked in this quest.

First, the scientific-technologically oriented culture tends to identify all solutions to problems as technical, functional and outside ourselves. The effects of this technically oriented culture I want to pursue further in the next section. This orientation tempts us when we talk about *the problem:* for some people it's the Bomb, for others it's the shelter, or Russian power, or Communist ideology; but it is more than likely that these things are not the problem at all but the consequences of the problem. There is a great temptation, though, if we find the problem in slogans, to seek the answer in slogans. Let's illustrate. If you are with a group of educated "problem-solvers" and say the problem is the Bomb, they will answer that the solution is more science and scientists; or if you say Africa, they will say more technicians; or say Russia, and they'll tell you we have to out-produce them.

Now these are not altogether false answers, but they are inadequate and inevitably too simple. We never presume that the problem is anywhere but outside us. It never seems to occur to us in our orientation that the trouble or the problem could be in man himself—the fact that we know everything about the world, the planet and its galaxies, but there is real ignorance about who *we* are in this universe. The world is to be studied, observed, analyzed but not experienced and felt.

Another obstacle to the exploration of inner space is the

tradition of a Calvinist-activist strain in our national character, represented by various names, including "the Protestant ethic." The basis of this emphasis was that the external world was to be captured for God, made over, transformed by men rearranging the economic, political and governing orders of the world. In this emphasis, industriousness, work and activity were divine attributes, while contemplation and leisure were tantamount to laziness and were works of the Devil. As a result, almost every American with this Protestant-Puritan strain in him finds pure leisure or quietude something to be avoided like the plague. Even the do-it-yourself fad, introduced as a form of leisure-time activity, became, under the impact of Calvinist activism, a thriving, bustling business which men pursue as if it were a second job.

A third block to this quest of inner space is the exteriorization of our lives in these contemporary times. We are an externalized people, active and outgoing to the extent that solitude is considered a morbidity of the worst kind. The exterior or the public has seeped through the dikes of our privacy until there is no seclusion left. We are going full tilt all the time; only in sleep do our lives become private; and even there the nightmares, our public fears and apprehensions disturb the only place of withdrawal left to us. We are public-minded, shut up outside ourselves, no longer at home. Perhaps that's why it takes so much to get through to us, to awaken a response in us. The headlines are larger, the commercials are louder, the politics more fanatical; our music shrieks, our paintings explode. We seem to be suffering from hypesthesia.

In this restless, violent time it is not easy to find some quiet, unbroken peace where we can gather the fragments of our scattered and disrupted existence. We have to find the time and the place to activate those higher and deeper sensibilities of our being lying unused. We must be awakened from the

stupor into which we have been drummed by the coarse
vulgarity of the colossal and the catastrophic; our feelings are
not beyond recovery. So much of life seems to lie trodden
under our scurrying feet, and the noisy novelties of everyday
cover the long-range dreams of a better and different kind of
life for each of us.

It is always easier to work on the world, but perhaps the
real work needs to be done with us. We need to be explored
down to our deepest needs. When Carl Sandburg finished his
biographies of Lincoln, someone asked him what he was
going to do. "I think," he replied, "I'd like to find out who
this fellow Sandburg is." If we think the frontier of outer
space presents some difficult obstacles, we haven't tried the
inner one. The uncharted wilderness of the inner person offers
a new challenge. M. Meister Eckhart described us:

A man has many skins in himself, covering the depths of his heart.
Man knows so many things; he does not know himself. Why,
thirty or forty skins or hides just like an ox's or a bear's so thick or
hard, cover the soul. Go into your own ground and know yourself
there.

Well, what will we discover in this new realm of inner space,
and what will be required of us in terms of equipment and
adjustment? What kind of knowledge will help us unriddle
the inner universe of man?

We will discover here that not all life is action, and that
in order to live in the world we will have to find time for
retreat and resignation, without feeling guilty or irresponsible.
Now, I am not suggesting any kind of Eastern mysticism or
religious otherworldliness but the necessary rhythm of existence which we in the Western world need to cultivate. To
practice an *external* speedup in this life without some kind of
internal slowdown is an extravagant misdirection of our time
and energy. We must learn that there are occasions when

resignation and inaction are the prerequisites of true existence
and to do nothing is the highest and most responsible form
of being (and I am not sure that this truth can ever pierce
the American armor of activism). Antoine de Saint-Exupéry in
his *Flight to Arras* says:

What are we worth when motionless is the question. There is a
density of being in a Dominican at prayer. He is never so much
alive as when prostrate and motionless before his God. In Pasteur,
holding his breath over the microscope, there is a density of being.
Pasteur is never more alive than in that moment of scrutiny. At that
moment he is moving forward. He is hurrying, he is advancing in
seven-league boots, exploring distance despite his immobility.
Cézanne, mute and motionless before his sketch, is an inestimable
presence. He is never more alive than when silent, when feeling and
pondering.

What will this resignation mean to us? It will mean the
cultivation of the practice of withdrawal—stepping out of the
rat race for a time and watching the wheel whir, to find out
what real differences that motion makes. It means we will have
to employ new disciplines and exercises that will confirm their
detachment from the prevalent customs and restore initiative
to the human spirit. Lewis Mumford talks about this kind of
withdrawal in his book, *The Conduct of Life:*

. . . (withdrawal) consists of little undramatic acts, hardly visible
even to your closest associates, concealed perhaps from your wife or
husband or your bosom friend: indeed it will be hard at first to convince yourself that anything so quiet, so modest in dimensions, so
unpublicizable, could bring about such a profound change. Yet
this very chastity and insignificance is perhaps what indicates it to
be a major break entirely out of the style of our existing society.
Epicurus's injunction, Hide thyself, is the first move toward having
an inner life.

The discipline of resignation or withdrawal will be very pain-
ful, because the treadmill of our daily life leads us to go
through so many involuntary motions. When we live in a

culture where external stimuli—the headline, the broadcast, the speech, the book (even this one)—replace the inner purposes of our lives, we drift from moment to moment, from hour to hour, from one lifetime to another without ever recovering the initiative. Where is the time and place when our myriad forms of action, the relentless pursuits of our lives are scrutinized and placed in some perspective? If we use this withdrawal for such an examination, we may discover how much of our lives has been covered over by conventional routine, and how little of our anxious activity and frenetic endeavor really arises from felt needs, clear convictions and intelligible and communicable purposes.

In this frontier of inner space, it will be necessary to carry on an inner dialogue with the self. Father Zossima in *The Brothers Karamazov* says, "Every day and every hour, every minute walk around yourself and watch yourself and see that your image is a seemly one." In a world where our lives are externalized and objectivized, it is one of the laws of self-preservation that this inner conversation must be much more highly developed in the human being if his spirit is to survive.

When man is truly human and has not been robbed of his birthright, there is an interior dialogue that never ceases; and the eternal questions in man's quest, and some of the answers, are there in the midst of the dialogue. The answers may be ringed around with a wraith of mystery so that there is an air of awe and wonder on the far side of each reply. Yet if they have scrutinized the living scene and given him a direction, a space in which to breathe and some clues that stop the contemplative ache, he has a world to live in as he searches for better ones. No matter how heavily any society may drug its members, either with threats of physical harm or with the anesthetics of physical plenty, in an effort to keep these queries under, there will always be those who will cry out and waken others, and the inner dialogue will go on.

If this dialogue is shut off or drowned out, life becomes desperately delimited. Before we are thirty we have that sense of being caught, and we lack the energies and tools to extricate ourselves from the debris blocking our return to life. That deficiency accounts for an almost unendurable boredom which hangs over our civilization; the mechanism busily purrs and ticks, but the days of the favored groups and classes are as empty as a handless clock. When the dialogue dies, our inner selves diminish, our self-confidence withers away, and we have a thousand minute questions about mechanisms and institutions around us. And a great deal of our energy goes into patchwork repairs and piecemeal reforms because we accept as fixed and unchangeable all the dominate tendencies of our culture.

These regions of inner space are a world with a new kind of time. Now we are a people tyrannized by time. We run our whole lives by the clock. It is the first thing we hear in the morning, the last thing we hear as we fall asleep at night. We go to work by the clock, take the train by the clock, eat by the clock. To be efficient you must time yourself, whether you are reading or traveling or cooking a meal. Soon we may be hearing about efficiency experts in love-making. Ours is a clock-obsessed age. But man does not live by the clock alone. The Greeks have two words for time: *chronos* which means clock time—calendar time, years, months, days, hours, minutes —all measurable lengths of time; the other word is *kairos,* and it means literally, high time, a time of decision, a meaningful time. We are slaves of *chronos*—we have clocks surrounding us and we live by the appointment book, but this is not the *real* time. We all spend time on this earth, a certain number of years and months and days, but that isn't what really matters. What is important is the *kairos*—the high time—the times in our life so filled with meaning and purpose that *chronos* doesn't seem to matter anymore.

Rollo May gives this illustration about a young man who

spent an hour traveling on a subway to his work, eight hours on his relatively uninteresting job, ten minutes after work talking to a girl he had recently fallen in love with, and two hours in the evening at an adult education class. Today he remembers nothing of the two hours on the subway; the eight hours on the job made little impression on him; of the evening class he can recall a little more. But the ten minutes with the girl occupies him most of all. It is not the length of time but the meaning of the time that matters.

These times of fulfillment are carriers of eternity. It is not a mere sterile timelessness, a cosmic stagnation, but the fullness of time. It is the "pregnant moment," like the time you first knew you were in love, or your first child was born, or that moment when you knew real freedom from everything and everyone that had enslaved you. Life can be studded with those timeless times, when eternity plants its gay banner and establishes a beachhead among the clocks and calendars.

I have only hinted at the potentials for the life of inner space. It will require perhaps a different kind of man, but, though man may be a "faulty construction" for flight into outer space, there is ample evidence that he is equipped for the frontiers of the inner world if he can just push aside all the blocks our contemporary culture puts in his way.

Necropolis and the New Jerusalem

Some Notes from Those Who Love Cities to Those Who Plan Them

UNDOUBTEDLY THERE ARE certain dynamics of a technological and industrial society that have helped to bring about the amazing growth of cities over the past five decades, but also there are probably psychological reasons that people rush to the large cities with a deep hunger to find the fulfillment the town or village never gave them. How else explain that in the great metropolises we are packing ourselves so close together the grass cannot grow under our feet, and the days and nights are filled with the ceaseless coming and going of millions of people? Here the pursuit of happiness, of meaning, of belonging is compounded by the franticness with which people pursue the common necessities of life. In speaking about the city I have no technical competence, but I have lived all my life in cities and have a deep love for them and am saddened by the way individual lives are blasted by the city. This tragedy does not all come as an inevitable by-product of masses of people living close together, but it does come, in part, from the plans, carefully laid out, for destroying and rebuilding cities. I do not wish to make city planners, or architects or city planning commissions the whipping boys of this discussion—they have come in for their share of criticism (much of it richly deserved)—but they, along with the people, are responsible for the chaotic state of our cities in the present time. We are at least 50 years late in our consciousness of urbanization.

However, we should not be surprised at the cultural lag in city planning and urban thinking when we realize that the United States is probably the most thoroughly antiurban nation in the world. Considerably more than half of our people live in cities and urban regions, yet the point of view, the value system and mythology of this nation are basically rural and village oriented. Even though the progress wheels of urbanization and industrialization have dragged us forward with considerable speed since the 1880's, our country has never come to grips with this significant fact of the twentieth century.

This antiurban attitude even receives a religious base for its prejudice. There is a saying that "man made the city, but God made the country." People talk about the city as though it were an adjunct of hell, and their true feeling is shown by their pity when they discover you live in the city. To them, feeling close to God or spiritual communion requires the country, some lake, or mountain or oceanside. Well, I love all these places of physical beauty, but they have no monopoly on speaking to our souls or arousing our aesthetic sensitivity.

Who has not been stirred by the sight of New York's skyline as one approaches it at dusk or by the dramatic appeal of Michigan Boulevard in Chicago with its juxtaposition of skyscrapers, traffic arteries, parks and lake? Or who could forget coming into San Francisco by steamer and seeing the beauty of the harbor encompassed by the city and overarched by one of the world's most beautiful manmade bridges? When listing mystical experiences let's not limit them to the Grand Canyon and Yosemite National Park.

But if this antiurban feeling is related to certain religious feelings and moralisms associated with rural and small-town values, we ought not to be surprised, for our whole social, political philosophy and literature are shot through with this same rejection or ignoring of the city—a feeling that the city somehow is not a fit habitat in which to live and rear our children. This is not a healthy symptom of the social and political growth of this nation. Morton and Lucia White, in their significant work, *The Intellectual Versus the City*, state it starkly for us:

We have no tradition of romantic attachment to the city in our highbrow literature, nothing that remotely resembles the Greek philosophers' attachment to the *polis* or the French writers' affection for Paris. . . . Throughout the nineteenth century our society was becoming more and more urbanized but the literary tendency to denigrate the American city hardly declined in proportion. If anything it increased in proportion.

We know from the writings of Thomas Jefferson that he hoped to arrest the development of the city in American life, because for him it was a "cancer" on the "body politic" in addition to being a physical and moral eyesore which would prove detrimental to American progress. Emerson agreed with Jefferson about the city, but rather than argue against the city in political terms, or agree with Jefferson's deprecation of the nasty manners and principles of the city, Emerson undergirded his feeling with metaphysical theory. There isn't time here to develop in detail this intellectual crop of antiurban feeling, but, in order to escape it, one would have to ignore Thoreau, Hawthorne, Melville, Poe, Henry Adams, Henry James, Louis Sullivan, Frank Lloyd Wright and John Dewey. In other words, we are the inheritors of a very dubious legacy that the city is tantamount to being godless and un-American. (If you think this is too strong, read the composite image of the city by the small-town residents of Springdale in Vidich's and Bensman's *Small Town in Mass Society*.)

It is little wonder therefore, that, though the rise of the cities was detected in the 1840's, there was no real attempt to deal with the city as an American social phenomenon until well into the twentieth century. There was no heritage but the rural, small-town one on which to build, accompanied by a deep anti-city mind-set. I would venture to guess, incidentally, that Mr. Kennedy is the first truly urban President we have had in the White House. It is also noteworthy that he received one of his first important setbacks when he gave more than lip service to his concern for the problems of urban life with his plan to include in his Cabinet a Department of Urban Affairs which was soundly beaten by agrarian America.

Now this antiurban prejudice would not be so important except for the fact that I believe this inheritance has created a serious vacuum in any kind of adequate base of presuppositions for city planning. It has left our planners a built-in antipathy for the city even as they planned, designed and attempted to rebuild it. The cultural lag which we spoke of earlier may be due to the fact that the city planner and urban reformer have a deep feeling that there is no important metaphysic or mystique on which to build his principles. Now far be it from me to offer a theology of city planning (even if I knew what it was), but I would like to suggest what I think some of the significant urban philosophers and thinkers have been saying about these presuppositions and their implications for the nature of the city, its housing, its parks, its centers, its peoples.

Before I turn to this task, I want to reveal a feeling which is basic to my acceptance of the city without overromanticizing it. It is this: that the story of every city is a "tale of two cities"; there are two sides to the city—it is a mixture of good and evil as life itself. We have seen this aspect of the city throughout human history. Every city has been a Babylon, every city a New Jerusalem. All cities have things that remind us of hell. In New York babies still have their throats cut by sewer rats; there are places where ten or more people live in a coalbin; there are women who have to sell themselves and pimps and pushers and junkies and precocious kids, wise to the ways of the streets at nine years of age. There are skid rows and black ghettos, and you will find the smell of death in the city, not of people dying but of a city deteriorating. A mayor of a large city says:

Decay is like a dagger at the heart of the city. It is evident even as the new projects we're planning failed even the basic need for safe and healthy living. It is apparent in the alleys that form an endless network, each harboring its own stories of human misery and deterioration. It is found in the noise and odors of business and industrial enterprises where people live—the stench of a decaying and dying city and the unchecked blight fans out in all directions, planting in healthy areas the seeds of decay.

Surely there is in every city a foretaste of necropolis, but this is no more the city than cancer is a man. Imperfection is the broken reflection of perfection. The city of destruction is a working model for the New Jerusalem, the city of life, albeit a clumsy and imperfect one, but sufficiently accurate to point to that which it temporarily prefigures.

Now with this I would like to turn to a consideration of what I have presumptuously called a metaphysic or mystique for the building of a city of life. This requires that we address ourselves to several aspects of the nature of the city and look at the insights and implications that these characteristics might throw upon planning and providing for the growth of cities.

I would like to suggest that the *city is sacramental.* The classic theological definition of that term is "an outward and visible symbol of an inward and spiritual meaning." The physical and material outline of the city, its visible structure and form, is the outward manifestation of that which it truly is— the soul of its people. If the city's only purpose is to house an inordinate amount of people or to build roads to accommodate a ridiculous amount of cars or to police and protect an ungovernable amount of human beings, then of course, let's decentralize now and make the job simple; but a city is more than that. Mumford, in *The City in History*, puts it succinctly for us:

We must restore to the city the material, life-nurturing functions, the autonomous activities, the symbiotic associations that have long been neglected or suppressed. For the city should be an organ of love; and the *best economy of cities is the care and culture of men*.

But not only the *"care and culture of men"*; this is not enough. A city at its best is a civilization in itself. This is the brightness and beauty of ancient Athens, and one of the reasons that it is still held up as a working model of the city. A civilized man is, by derivation of the word, one who lives and thinks in the city. Such a "civilized" man could only be produced in the cities of an earlier age that were communities. It is the functions a city performs that make it a civilization. An important thing for the planner to keep in mind is the way in which the physical and material planning for the city enables its people to create a civilization. If a city is true to its nature, it will be complete and whole; it will be generating and creating a civilization, and this, in part, will distinguish it from an urban conglomeration.

The experts who plan and govern cities must ask if their tasks and the way in which they perform them are enabling men to be complete human beings. Cities do run through cycles—there is a law of obsolescence, and slums, disease, decay and delinquency have to be dealt with—there are the symptoms of civic immorality (the revelations of the housing scandals in New York City in the past five years are symbolic of a complete breakdown in civic conscience). The only adequate reason for rebuilding of the city is in order that men may be civilized and the city's humanity restored. It is to our eternal discredit that "urban renewal" in the recent past seldom coincided with this objective. We have seemed to be either dedicated to carefully planning monuments to massiveness or carelessly letting our cities sprawl aimlessly in disconnected entities over the countryside, thus destroying all cohesiveness and community. In both instances, human beings become the objects that make up cities rather than subjects for which and around whom cities should be built.

There is great evidence that the thesis of Mrs. Jane Jacobs in her concluding chapter in *The Death and Life of Great American Cities* is all too true; namely, that the city planners and philosophers of city planning have approached the city from the viewpoint of the physical sciences in which cities were seen as "problems in disorganized complexity, understandable purely by statistical analysis, predictable by the application of probability mathematics, manageable by conversions into groups of averages." And out of this mentality has come the demolition of neighborhoods that destroyed communities and broke the fabric of human interrelationships; the creation of large traffic arteries that helped the flow of cars but bisected, mutilated, and isolated neighborhoods; the clearing of large patches of space and light called parks that are unused and nonfunctional.

The true "civitas" has an economy, a culture, a civilization that grows out of the interaction of the spirits of its people. It does not matter how tall our buildings are, how capacious our apartment houses, how extensive our public-housing projects, how imposing our office buildings. It is not the size of our cities that matters but the kind of life we are able to live in them, not the mountain of manufactured goods that flows in and out of its industries but the kind of men created in the process, not bank clearings but abundant life. T. S. Eliot puts the question to us in his chorus from "The Rock":

Though you have shelters and institutions,
Precarious lodgings where the rent is paid,
Subsiding basements where the rat breeds
Or sanitary dwellings with numbered doors . . .

When a Stranger says: "What is the meaning of this city?
Do you huddle together because you love each other?"
What will you answer? "We all dwell together
To make money from each other"? or "This is a community"?

The physical city is the form of its civilization. It is sacramental—the city is a material manifestation of an invisible
reality.

The city is symbiotic relations. The biological meaning of
the word symbiotic is the "living together in intimate associa-
tion of dissimilar organisms." This characteristic lies deep at
the heart of the city and its true nature. One of the city's most
marvelous gifts is that of people, thousands of them who con-
gregate—the amazing richness and diversity of people, the
contrast of so many varied colors and shades of skin, the
strangeness and familiarity of all kinds of languages, the
never-ending variety of human faces etched with care and
suffering, with tribulation, joy, hope and happiness. There can
be no civilization without this essential fact—a diversity of
humanity as well as facilities and centers of culture. We are
all aware that there has been a steady eradication of this diversity of human beings at neighborhood, district and city-wide
levels. We are rapidly becoming a two-class city of the very
poor and the very wealthy; those who live in luxury dwellings
and those who live in tenements. The great middle has been
distributed in the green belt at great loss to the city.

The city needs, in order to be a city, the heterogeneous population of persons from *every* socioeconomic background; the
more ethnic and cultural diversity a city houses, the richer it
will be in its offering. The same way a city plans for diversity
of land uses through its zoning laws, it must also plan (and
plan wisely) for a diversity of humanity in neighborhoods and
communities. But whether premeditated or not, our cities are
planned for the destruction of diversity. In housing, for example, we make sure that there is no mixture of income groups,

sentencing all those of low-income range to vast areas of un-relieved sameness called housing projects. More often than not, this project is not only a low-income ghetto, but a racial and ethnic ghetto as well. The tragic note is that these are not the accidental groupings of people who huddle together competitively in the race for low rents; this is the *destruction of diversity by design.*

One of the hopeful signs on the horizon of urban planning is the intention to include in some projected urban renewal projects gradations of income housing all the way from low-income public housing to upper-middle—all located in the same slum clearance program. Every public encouragement should be given to this important principle to see that it receives practical implementation.

The heterogeneity of a great city may have been spontaneous and somewhat accidental in its beginning, but it will remain so only by wise and intelligent planning. The city must protect diversity wherever it thrives, nurture it wherever it is a potential, and build for it. Every neighborhood and district must be conscious and jealous of its diversity, ever alert to each destructive tendency which seems to presume that it would be desirable if "those people" were not next door to us, or on our street. In Greenwich Village we have an interesting and somewhat insidious illustration of the lack of appreciation of diversity. Periodically we have a campaign sponsored by several leading citizens and businessmen to divest our neighborhood of "derelicts" and "indigents." This campaign is carried on by appealing for an economic boycott—"don't give money to the bums"—in the hope that the financial famine will send them to greener pastures.

I feel deeply resentful of this kind of organized drying up of the milk of human kindness which flows far too little in our impersonal world. Besides I think it wrong to send these people away; we need them as they need us. The derelict reminds us of what we might be or really are even with our good jobs and middle-class values and self-respect—that we, like him, may be at the end of our rope but with a few more illusions to insulate us. It is possible for us to keep going in a well-kept, well-clothed, and well-fed emptiness. We must learn to value the place of every kind of human being, rich and poor, success and failure, beat and square, white and black, ugly and beautiful. If the city passes laws, plans land uses, builds housing so as to vitiate the principle of diversity, of these symbiotic relations, then the self-destruction of the city has begun.

Before concluding this section, I want to mention one form of symbiotic relations highly dangerous and detrimental to the life of our city. It is known as negative symbiosis and parasitism. In the city there are people who live excessively and immorally off their relationships with others. The most obvious example is the slumlord of urban deteriorated housing—that whipping boy of campaigning politicians and crusading newspapers. Now, I'm not defending slumlords; but, if I'm not sadly mistaken, there are laws on the books of the state and city of New York which have made such parasitism not only desirable but highly profitable. With such respectable legal and financial encouragement, it's hard for a man to resist the temptation to live off the misery and degradation of his fellowman. We who create the laws must see to it that parasitism is not rewarded with money.

The city as drama and dialogue. One of the most interesting themes that Mumford develops in his *City in History,* is the concept of the urban drama. The development of the city and drama go hand in hand. In fifth-century Athens, the *ecclesia* was a great agon or contest of statesmen, and there were contests of potters, of horse breeders, singers, composers and dramatists. The practice of choosing leaders and taking sides was one of the earliest forms of social differentiations. The city magnified this process and multiplied its occasions.

The city actually became a vast theater housing a drama of inestimable proportions. For in the city a "full cast of characters could be assembled and there were sufficient diversity and competition to enliven the plot and bring the performance up to the highest pitch of skilled, intensely conscious participation."

Now it is Mumford's contention that the great dramatic occasions of urban life, the courtroom, the arena, the parliament, the council meeting, are what give meaning and values to so much of the activities of the city. Out of this ritual and dramatic action has come the dialogue—the ultimate expression of city life. The first urban communities were only monologues—a priest or royal one gave the orders and there was no reply. But dialogue was the first step out of tribal conformity, and it challenged the dead unanimity of centralized absolutism. Haemon in Sophocles' *Antigone* says "a city that is of one man only is no city." Only where differences are heard and valued, and opposition tolerated, can struggle be transmuted into the dialectic—the dialogue of the city. Let me quote one very significant statement from Mumford's thesis:

And if provision for dialogue and drama, in all their ramifications, is one of the essential offices of the city, then one key to urban development should be plain—it lies in the widening circle of those capable of participating until in the end all men will take part in the conversation.

In a sense, therefore, the dramatic dialogue is one of the fullest symbols of what the city is and has important implications for those who are planning its future.

Let's look at the city today to see what has happened to the dialogue. Two important and interrelated changes have served to deafen the dialogue and deaden the drama, namely *growth* and the *shift of power*. This is true of every American city, but let's take New York as an example. It covers three-hundred square miles packed with eight million people. The city's budget is two billion dollars. The police force numbers over 24,000 men. Altogether there is a municipal work force of 220,000. The sheer weight of people crowded together in the metropolis, the tremendous size of the bureaucracy, and the enormous power wielded by the multimillion-dollar budget all point to the problem of the shift in power.

The prime way in which the power structure in the city has changed is that now the power rests primarily at the *top* which is cut off in a serious way from the public to which it belongs. I think it would be valuable to turn to one of the analyses of C. Wright Mills in his chapter on "The Mass Society" in *The Power Elite*. In assessing what has happened to structures in urban society, he makes the point that the growth of the metropolis atomized community, and the growth of bureaucracy thrusts decision-making centers beyond the effective range of understanding and influence, leaving the individual isolated and exposed. Mills expressed his evaluation about the metropolis in this way:

The growth of the metropolis segregating men and women into narrowed routines and environments causes them to lose any firm sense of integrity as a public. The members of publics in smaller communities know each other more or less fully because they meet in several aspects of the total life routine. The members of masses in a metropolitan society know one another only as fractions in specialized milieux. . . . *In every major area of life the loss of the sense of structure and the submergence into powerless milieux is the cardinal fact.* In the great city the division of milieux and the segregating routines reach the point of closest contact with the individual and the family, for although the city is not the limit of prime decision, even the city cannot be seen as a total structure by most of its citizens.

It is the inaccessibility of the structures of power in the city that makes the average citizen feel so unable to take action. Mills illustrates this importance of structural relevancy by talking of unemployment. For example, if a handful of men do not have jobs and will not seek work, we look for the cause of the situation in the character of the person. But when twelve million men are unemployed, they can't all be "lazy" and "no good." Economists call this "structural unemployment," meaning that the men involved can't control their job opportunities. In fact, there is little *one* man in *one* place can do about it when it sweeps over his personal existence.

The foregoing illustrates the structural relationship of the individual and the public to the power mechanism in the city; the individual is so far removed from it there seems no way to understand it or affect it, and one man in one part of the city can do little about it.

The consequences of this are obvious. Everywhere one goes he hears protests against injustice or corruption or inequities in which people talk about "they." "They" are raising taxes; "they" are demolishing the city until nothing will be left but high-rise luxuries and low-rise tenements; "they" are conspiring against the public. The use of "they" symbolizes the basic feeling of detachment from the process of governing. Fred Cook, a reporter, put it thus:

. . . [there is a] sharp cleavage between the congested and struggling and essentially helpless millions and the lives of an official and business aristocracy which has lost virtually all its old connections with the grass roots. If it was true that in the old Boston that the Cabots spoke only to the Lowells and the Lowells spoke only to God, it is even more true in today's New York that power speaks only to power and no further.

Some urban statesman has rightly said that the next big concern for the city electorate is how to "curb the bureaucrats, how to keep the experts under control and how to keep them from making all the decisions." This battle transcends all partisan and political interests and will require an alert and concerned citizenry. The battle has already begun in cities all over the nation and memorial battlegrounds are springing up, sometimes streets, sometimes housing projects, sometimes parks. One of the best-known battlegrounds is New York's Washington Square Park where the lines have been drawn time and again. Though the issues have varied, the principle is the same: the dialogue must be resumed; the people who live in and use the city must be allowed to participate in the decisions that affect the future of their neighborhood and district; and the monologue of power and planning must cease.

Washington Square Park in Greenwich Village is such a symbol. The past few years have seen a running battle between officialdom and the citizenry.

In 1958, the plans on the drawing boards of the Planning Commission in New York City became public knowledge—a plan to split Washington Square Park with a major roadway, continuing Fifth Avenue south of the park. Without any prior consultation with the Village community, the powers that be planned their mutilation and partition of the park. When the community learned of the plan and were apprised of its consequences, there arose one of the most united and successful community organization campaigns ever to let City Hall and all its departments hear the people. The battle continued over a period of several years, finally culminating in the closing of the park to all traffic and a proposed rehabilitation of the area. The sounds of the people's voices, like Greek choruses, are getting louder and more frequent in cities all over this country.

The threat presented by all omniscient planners is that sometimes they suffer from the delusion that in their egocentric bias or in their self-confident mastery of theory and expertise they know what is best for all people and communities. This crystal-ball insight into all people's needs generally suffers from an inevitable parochialism that makes dialogue, that is community consultation, so necessary.

The lack of the dialogue and significant and meaningful places and ways in which the drama can be played out is the reason we have politics by pressure and picket lines and planning commission meetings punctuated by the cries of an outraged citizenry with the result that many times the noisiest crowd gets the best hearing. If we may listen to Mumford again, he says:

The most revealing symbol of the city's failure, of its very non-existence as a social personality, is the absence of dialogue, not necessarily a silence but equally the loud sound of a chorus utter-ing the same words in cowed if complacent conformity. . . . Such a drama is bound to have a fatal last act.

Another characteristic of the city is that *it is finite and passing*. Whatever may be our position on the finitude of man (and I think there are few who want to argue for our infinite durability), I believe it almost impossible for us to accept the fact that the cities we have planned and built will pass away. Though most of us have heard of the dire predictions about necropolis and have visited those inner ecological areas with the smell of decay about them, I don't believe we can see in our mind's eye the Empire State Building's half-sized stat-uary overgrown and standing mute testimony to what once was a thriving city; or to see the thoroughfares and main arter-ies of the cities as asphalt paths with weeds and grass growing through the cracks.

Perhaps there is a need for a new study among builders and planners called "urban eschatology." It could bring to planning a much needed humility. To stand before the precariousness of all that is planned and built and to realize that as for cities there is a beginning so also there is an end, would be a sobering exercise. If serious reflection were given to this by the builders of and the dwellers in cities, we might be able to understand Robert Nichols' poem, "The City."

I sing of the city revived. Citizen, I cry to you in favor of integration and municipal reconstruction. It is time that you reckoned up the cost of your own follies.

Consider: a city wasted at the guts like present-day Detroit, or like Carthage, Zabae or ancient Tun Huang whose market stalls have crumbled into dust and whose main squares have become the stony pasture for goats.

With the receding of the third, seventh and eighteenth waves of traffic, the lungs of the metropole have been pumped dry. Nothing is left but old postal routes, cracked mains, and monuments torn from their plinths lying among the hardhack and huckleberry-species which seem to readily colonize these burned-out areas.

The spirit of applied mathematics broods. All surfaces bear the glacial traces of cars. The wheel has described its double arabesque, its exquisite compound parabola, on a field of bare snow.

Children play among the debris. They climb barefoot among the fashionable used brick and antique doorknobs salvaged from the old Murray Hill Hotel. A small replica of the Gulf Oil building has been reconstructed out of rusted beer cans. The Jumel Mansion has been reassembled out of the shards of cracked flower pots.

Parades are held. Chlorophyll has become scarce. Gigantic mushrooms inflated with helium are pulled through the charcoal streets. On the cornices of the public library, lime-gatherers are at work.

In the main gathering place, which is called "Mauve Square," a statue has been set up in memory of Monochrome, who has devoted a large part of his very considerable fortune during the past years towards the rediscovery of pigment. His factories have been opened to the blind of all ages, who work there without discrimination, and in the most agreeable circumstances.

Already three of the six known primary colors have been synthesized, and it is confidently predicted that the entire spectrum, as it was originally worked out, will be rediscovered during the next decades.

Now we are getting somewhere. Come with me. Drive through these sunken streets which have been recently reclaimed from the New Jersey marshlands by the Department of Marine and Aviation. One moves at a snail's pace against the crowd of tourists and melancholy drifters, as if breasting some tangible current. The door of the taxi opens. One is escorted down the three steps of "Le Negre Diabetique" by the chasseur. Or sit at the window of your favorite pre-Raphaelite cafe among the ruins, and watch humanity as it goes by. A whole geography could be guessed at, if there were space. If there were but room!

Deadbeats from all over the world have been assembled, drawn by the smell of chocolate and by the pornographic pictures nailed by the Chamber of Commerce over the open cellar holes, from which music vibrates. The last cowpunchers are here. Refugees from the Tong Wars. The residuary legatees of the Zuni Indians have come in search of libraries. A new order of nomadic tribesmen from the raw steppes have been drawn by the chain laundries and prospects in the chemical dye industry.

An unbelievable profusion. From particles of these faces, from sections of these gaits, gestures, inflections, as well as from an examination of hair and bits of teeth, reconstruct if you will the Great Plain. And from modes of ornament and characteristic ways of elongating and flattening certain bones, plot the limit of the Frontier.

Space recaptured! Urbs! The full Plenum!

It has just begun to dawn on people, though we do not talk about it freely as yet, that the city—New York City and every other one—is utterly destructible. Those intimations of mortality are no longer that, but broad, suggestive hints of the future. Not only may cities die from instant megatons; they will expire when their decay outstrips their renewal, even though they may continue to look as if they are alive and growing. It ought to be understood by those who plan cities, those who govern them, and those who live in them that a city may be destroyed by the push of a button, but it also may die of soul rot which is worse. A city may die when it no longer creates civilized men, when it destroys diversity in the humanity that occupies it, and when it debilitates the dialogue that makes for true drama.

A city is dying when it has an eye for real-estate values

but no heart for personal values; when it has an understanding about traffic flow but no concern about the flow of human beings; when we have building codes but little time for ethical codes. When these values are absent at the heart of decision-making and planning and governing, the city is dead and all that is left is decay.

The vision that has stirred the conscience of man for centuries and moves us today is the vision of an eternal city; we do not yet know it in time and space. The city described in the ancient story is one where there are no tears, no mourning, no death. It is an incredible and unbelievable vision and, though we do not have it, we have at least the outlines of a city of life for which we can dream and build. The conflict and paradox of the city are the same as those in the life of every citizen, and the struggle to build a new city is the same as creating for each of ourselves a new kind of life.

The Forsakedness of the Young

THERE IS PERHAPS no group in our culture so affected by the repercussion of this strange new age we live in as the younger generation. In many ways they have been the most exposed to the impact without any of the protection the older generation had grown up in. I cannot completely sympathize with the members of this younger generation because I am that awkward age, having been born in the generation between "the lost" and "the beat."

However, in spite of these problems, I have spent the last twenty years working and living with and counseling youth. Out of these experiences have grown some convictions I want to share. Right off I want to state my bias. I resent the seriousness behind the repeated query, what's the matter with kids today? We have short memories, don't we? We forget the Roaring Twenties and the untouchables, the depressive thirties and the lines of hunger. We forget that Buchenwald, Hiroshima, and the Yalu River are names we made famous. After all, we built the world they inherited. We try to make the young act the way we don't. Teach them to be polite and generous and to believe in the sacred dignity of every human being. But they are wise; they look around and see the disheartening "facts of life," that ultimately individuals and nations use violent force to solve their problems, and that in a crisis individuals must be sacrificed to a machine, or the state or an institution. Little wonder we find distrust, cynicism and apathy in the young.

Alfred Whitehead describes the eternal struggle between the old and the young: We may conceive humanity as engaged in an internecine conflict between youth and age. Youth is not defined by years but by the creative impulse to make something. The aged are those who before all things, desire not to make a mistake. Logic is the olive branch from the old to the young. I think we can understand why the young refuse this symbol of peace, for they must be allowed to feel, to scent, to presage, to fight for themselves, before we can speak to them logically.

In order to understand we must review some of the influences impinging on the younger generation, with the resulting tensions and conflicts. First, I would like to mention the historical background of this younger generation. It may help us to recall just how far removed we are from this present generation of youth. They were born and weaned in the midst of global war—their formative months spent in the midst of familial upheaval, of life broken by separation of father and mother; the days of puberty were passed during strange wars called "hot" and "cold," and their brothers and fathers turned up dead at the end of a telegram.

They grew to adolescence in the midst of a historical climate of violence and tremulous insecurity. The cataclysms of wars, the dwindling hopes of peace, the social and political revolution out of which new nations were born, the rising tides of nationalism and racialism shook the orderly foundation of the way things were. All the conventional concepts of private and public ethics atrophied under the constant exposure of thievery, bribery and even treason in high and low places. It was a time when the science-fiction world of Buck Rogers and Jules Verne burst into fact. This generation became the first to be totally exposed to the mass media, living almost exclusively off secondhand reports about life.

In recent centuries no young people seem to have been

confronted by such foundation-shaking and anxiety-producing circumstances facing the young today. There was something steadier about the past which exerted its control and restraint on the nurture of the young. The corroding insecurities of today eat into the personal fibers of our youth in such a special way, I think we should marvel that so many do plan and conduct their lives, provide for their future and take life seriously; and that only an understandable minority of miscreants find their "kicks" in junk, fast cars, wild parties, and promiscuous and perverted sex.

The preoccupation of our adult world with the latter indicates more about us than it does about our "young." I think we are all suffering from a frenetic anxiety not just about our "flaming youth" or the "beat generation" but about ourselves, about what we believe and the way we live, about the new world into which we have been catapulted—both the physical world of outer space and the equally unfamiliar world taking shape before our eyes under the growing impact of automation, extended life and leisure, and overorganization. We need to appreciate the impact of these developments upon today's children and realize that the historical period in which the young have grown to maturity vitally affects their lives.

One evidence of our lack of comprehension is the way in which the adult world assesses the young and views their individual and collective actions; the way in which parents, police, social workers and ministers are downright shocked at the behavior of this present generation. We dwell on their behavior, moan over their crazy and irrational actions, raise an eyebrow or lower the boom on their sexual looseness, view with horror the addict hooked on heroin. The adults never seem to be able to see beyond the youth's action to the motivations and meaning of his behavior. Why is this? Perhaps because the adults harbor a nauseous fear that, at the bottom of it all, they will discover their own valueless and meaningless universe, the crazy-mixed-up world they bequeathed to the young, carried to its logical conclusion in the behavior of their children. Parents or any adults in authority who have seen that opaque nonlistening look come over the faces of the young are being exposed to the deepest sentiment of a generation that has been handed an adult world that is in many ways senseless and hypocritical.

It would do the older generation a lot of good to muster the kind of honesty expressed by a thief and former preacher in George Bernard Shaw's play, *Too True To Be Good:*

But how are we to bear this dreadful new nakedness, the nakedness of the souls who until now have always disguised themselves from one another in beautiful, impossible idealisms to enable them to bear one another's company? The iron lightning of war has burnt great rents in these angelic veils. . . . Our souls go in rags now; and the young are spying thru the holes and getting glimpses of the reality that was hidden. And they are not horrified: they exult in having found us out; they expose their own souls and when we, their elders, desperately try to patch our torn clothes with scraps of the old material the young lay violent hands on us and tear from us even the rags that were left to us. But when they have stripped themselves and us utterly naked will they be able to bear the spectacle?

The young have ways of exposing our idols and all the social lies by which we rationalize and protect ourselves from the internal collapse of our souls, and they have been immensely helped by the historical revolutions. The young were nurtured by this apocalyptic universe, so they do not believe the yarns we spin about superior "modern times" or inevitable progress. They are no longer interested in conquering the world; instead they don't want the world to conquer them. Certain things seem to be missing—the wildness of the "lost generation," the lyricism of the publicized "beats." There is nothing but a singular, obstinate search for happiness, free from illusion and ideological excesses of all types and carved out of the universal pessimism of nuclear catastrophe. They are not buying any utopias or systems that promise them happiness—they neither speculate about nor demand the "perfect world." There are no philosophical or literary heroes amongst our young. Perhaps the exception is J. D. Salinger who more than any other man seems to "turn on" the younger generation. I think there is good reason for this; Holden Caulfield exposes the "bad faith" of the adult world—all the expedient phoniness and pretense with which we spoil human interrelations. The literary critic, Nathan Scott, commenting on the deep resentment of Holden toward people, says:

And what really he is set on edge by is the insincerity, the evasiveness and the bad faith that are revealed in our common speech. For at the bottom the intensity and the wild erraticism of this boy are a profound sadness and embarrassment over the ugly slum of the human spirit that the world appears to be.

I believe the young identify with this deep feeling and are demanding our honesty and openness about our relationships with others as well as a probing of the great social lies that we pass off as universal customs necessary for survival. The young have developed a posture of "temporary skepticism" about all rational explanations and philosophical systems, and this will protect them from the erosions of disillusionment that were part of the older generation's experience.

We need to look beneath the surface of drag races, juvenile delinquency, "pot" parties, rock 'n' roll, the "twist," and all other publicized and sensational activities of the younger generation, if we are to understand the way they genuinely feel about the world they have been handed or the place in it that they inherited. It seems there are several basic prerequisites to a healthy relationship of the young to the society of which he is part. These prerequisites are part of the spoken and unspoken, conscious and unconscious needs of every maturing person.

First, the longing for identity, for a clear self-image. More than any other time in recent history, our young are suffering from the lack of self-identity. If certain elements are lacking in a person's diet, he is susceptible to so-called "deficiency diseases." There are many troubled youngsters, some on the verge of delinquent behavior and emotional disturbances, who are suffering from another kind of deficiency disease. They have been crippled by an inadequate concept of themselves—a distorted self-image. In adolescence they are still rummaging around in the attics of their subconscious for some clue as to who they are. In urban centers we have seen the growth of "street corner society," the name given to the delinquent subculture which becomes another substitute relationship in which the teen-agers seek to recover their identity. Even the image of a noisy, aggressive "cat" is better than no image at all.

I remember a young boy of the streets, with whom we have a working relationship, telling me in the jazzed-up jargon of his generation, "Look man, you don't dig my problems at all, like I'm on a big search for me and like, man, you ain't got a hint in this world where I oughta look but, nothin' is gonna hang me up, til' I find out."

A young graduate of Vassar, daughter of a wealthy New York family, said with no bitterness in her voice, "My folks gave me everything I could have wanted except one thing—they forgot to tell me who I was. What's the use of having money and education and friends if you don't know who has them?"

And then on a recent CBS report, called "A Volcano Named White," a young Negro in the death cell for murdering several innocent people without cause spoke of his early childhood in these pathetic words, "I remember my mother, but there were several fathers or people said they was my father but I couldn't find out who I was." No matter what the status in life, the longing and need for identity seem to be universal in this generation in a more peculiar way than ever before.

Secondly, the young deeply desire satisfactory relationships with adult persons, and this is closely related to the preceding problem. I have been associated with many predelinquent and delinquent children in the city, and it is my belief that most kids in trouble have never been able to have *any* satisfying relationship with an adult person, and yet they are forced continually to live and move and sustain themselves in a completely adult world. The distorted or lack of self-image, resulting from their own primary family situation, leads to the conflict with adults in every situation. These youths expect from *all* adult relationships the lovelessness, rejection, and anxiety that marked those of their early life. Consequently they do not really believe that adults will accept them.

The growth of all the subcultures, such as "bopping gangs," "coffeehouse cliques," secret societies, with private jargon and new values, seem to be an outward manifestation of the inability of the young to be at home in a society where adults have the dominating role and where the young have no place or voice in creating and shaping it.

Thirdly, beneath the surface of the seeming disbelief and immorality of the young, there is a *revolt* against the "meaningless and valueless" world. Appalled by their strange behavior, shocked by the chances they take, puzzled by the irrational nature of their crimes, the adult world throws up its hands in horror. Commenting on particularly bizarre and meaningless crimes committed by some teen-agers against an old and helpless man, John Clellon Holmes had a very provocative thesis about this kind of crime without passion, murder without motive. In an *Esquire* article, Holmes said this is the worst crime envisaged by the Marquis de Sade a hundred fifty years ago—a crime which the cruel absence of God makes obligatory if a man were to prove that he was a man and not a mere blot of matter. "Such crimes cannot be understood if we go on mouthing the same old panaceas about broken homes, slum environments and bad company—for they are spiritual crimes against the identity of another human being—crimes which reveal with terrifying reality the lengths to which a desperate need for values can drive the young."

Beneath the surface of their big talk, we need to examine the metaphysical mood of the younger generation, for it is one with an obsessive craving to believe, but it seems as ill equipped as any to satisfy his desire. The "temporary skepticism" of which we spoke earlier modifies all commitments. If a "beat" in a coffeehouse, drunk on existential despair, cries out his Nietzschean defiance that "God is dead," his young companions are just as likely to doubt the demise of the Divinity as they are to call in question the claims of the pious preacher in the pulpit who pretends to know God intimately and have a pipeline to His every move. Even the hard-core delinquent is lost in his unbelief. In a recent book about them called *The Sins of Their Fathers*, Marjorie Rittwagen, staff psychiatrist of New York City's Children's Court, speaking of teen-agers in trouble, says: "What I *have* seen by the hundreds, are miserable youngsters. Miserable, weak, fearful, inadequate, drifting children—without roots, without beliefs, without interests, without ambition. . . . It was this quality of 'emptiness,' the nothingness of many of these children that shocked me most. In a group, a class or a street gang they might be noisy and aggressive, but alone they had the defeated, beaten air of the very old, the very discouraged, the very hopeless."

In a remarkably sensitive article in *Dissent* magazine, describing a series of meetings with the youth of a bopping gang in the Bedford-Stuyvesant section of Brooklyn, Norman Mailer puts his finger on a very important vacuum in the lives of these youngsters:

For all the talk of broken homes, sub-marginal housing, over-crowding in the schools and cultural starvation, the other root is more alive, and one kills it at one's peril. It is the root for which our tongues once found the older words of courage, loyalty, honor and the urge for adventure. It may be that when one gets to know them well, some of the Dealers are bad pieces of work, but I would gamble that most of them are rather good pieces of work, bright, sensitive to what is true and what is not true in what you say to them, loyal if they like you, and in congress together they are as alive as a pack of monkeys. They suffer from only one disease, the national disease—it is boredom. If their conversation runs the predictable river-bed of sex, gang war, drugs, weapons, movies and crazy drunks, well, at least they live out a part of their con-versational obsession, which is more than one can say for the quiet, inhibited, middle-aged desperadoes of the corporation and the suburb. If we are to speak of shadows which haunt America today, the great shadow is that there is a place for everybody in our country who is willing to live the way others want him to, and talk the way others want him to, with our big, new, thick, leaden vocabulary of political, psychological, and sociological verbiage. Yes, there is a place for everybody now in the American scene except for those who want to find the limits of their growth by a life which is ready to welcome a little danger as part of the Divine cocktail.

Little wonder that we reap the whirlwind of hatred, hostility and violence in the lives of kids we permit to enter the world without the anchors of hope and meaning, or knowledge of good or evil.

For those who would look beyond the mere surface behavior of the young, it will become apparent that some of the needs and motivations already discussed account for many of their actions. I now want to turn to the themes of *resignation* and *rebellion* as significant problems in contemporary youth. *We have robbed the young of the power of rebellion, and we have condemned resignation as apathy and conformity.* Most of us were self-styled rebels in our youth, and we think of ourselves, even now, as bucking some kind of religious, social or political status quo. Hardly any of us would think of ourselves as "rebels without a cause"; we all have had our causes (both real and imaginary) which we have hugged closely to our bosoms and nursed in righteous indignation. We have manned the barricades of revolution against all kinds of conservatism and reactions. We wear the badge of rebellion proudly for all to see, and, albeit we are a little tired, and the badge a little tarnished, we still take umbrage at any slight questioning of the authenticity of our rebellion.

But what of the younger generation? What will he rebel against? Rebellion against the father, the family, religion, insofar as they represent tradition, the past and coercive authority, is absolutely necessary to growth and maturity. But what happens when a culture carefully removes all the objects of rebellion—ejects the authority, eliminates hard ethical choices, and takes away the tyranny of arbitrary demands? Then we deprive the young of a real necessity of life. I heard with interest the words of one sensitive father who said that his high-school-aged son claimed that the father's generation had robbed his of the possibilities of revolt. He sees clearly enough that for his young son the revolutionary gesture would be an empty piece of mimicry, incongruous in a world which has found there is no apocalypse and where contemporary society threatens not exclusion and failure, but acceptance and success. The single new slogan available to his son's generation is a pitiful one: "Get off my back." The father conjectured, "They should be on ours." Edgar Friedenberg in his remarkable book, *The Vanishing Adolescent,* underscores this dilemma in these words:

What adults call rebellion today is not . . . Today's youngster may be enraged but he is no rebel, because he is enraged not at the tyranny of adults but at their blandness, their weakness, their emptiness. He has no faith in the legitimacy of authority; he has never experienced authority. He may very well have experienced brutality at the hands of people who believed they were exercising authority; this must certainly have confirmed his suspicions that they did not know what it was. During the beating they showed no feeling; afterward they took no responsibility. They just left you alone with nothing to rebel for and nothing to rebel against except the feeling that you are nothing, too.

Mr. Friedenberg has put his finger on a highly important factor in the actions of the younger generation. Our danger is not that we are going to produce too many rebels but that we have made true rebellion impossible for the young. The temptation of the young will be to panic in their quest for authority and to make all kinds of mistakes about where to find it.

With rebellion dead or at least its possibilities seriously diminished, where should the young turn but to *resignation*, a pose written off as conformity by the same Calvinist, industrious, American activists we spoke of earlier. Resignation smacked to us of passiveness, mysticism, retreat and other-worldliness, and adults chided the young with taunts of "apathy" and "cowardice." But the real message of this new posture of the younger generation hasn't gotten through to us yet—the apolitical, asocial, aorganization spirit has not permeated the hyperactivated mentality in which we have been immersed. We are going to have to learn the *attributes* of resignation. If rebellion teaches us something about ourselves, helps us mature as individuals, frees us from fetters that have bound our lives, then passivity and resignation may also be a means of self-revelation. The history of the Jewish people is full of waiting patiently, resigned in some Egypt of their exile, because rebellion had no meaning or relevance. Waiting, whether for God or Godot or the healing passage of time, could bring us some new knowledge of who we are in this world. Albert Schweitzer has a meaningful word on this matter in his *Out of My Life and Thought*:

True resignation consists in this: that man, feeling his subordination to the course of world-happenings, wins his way to inward freedom from the fortunes which shape the outward side of his existence. . . . Resignation, therefore, is a spiritual and ethical affirmation of one's own existence. Only he who has gone through the stage of resignation is capable of world-affirmation.

I have a feeling that this younger generation is going to be much less incredulous of and much more at home with the prayer of Alcoholics Anonymous than we were:

> O Lord, grant me the serenity to accept
> the things I cannot change,
> The courage to change the things I can,
> And the wisdom to know the difference.

I think it is worth noting that one of the most effective means of social action or rebellion in our time is a *sit-in*, which is itself a form of resignation and submission. The shame of the adult world is that we have knowingly and unknowingly robbed the young of both rebellion and resignation.

The betrayal I think is most pointedly put when we recognize that when adults look at the young and their actions, we do not see the young at all—their needs, aspirations, longings—adults see only in their behavior their own hopes and fears and project onto the youth their anxieties and neuroses. Mr. Friedenberg, quoted earlier, has a very interesting thesis concerning this. He suggests that adult response to the way the young act seems to be more highly influenced by the adults' own unconscious needs and tensions than by what the young are doing. Some of the adult feelings come from the fear that the adolescent will get out of the adult's control and throw out of control other situations in which the adult is involved; the latent hostility at the virility and youthfulness of adolescence while we are aging; and the envy of the life not yet squandered and fouled up by mistakes and circumstances. All of these, Mr. Friedenberg suggests, are unconscious factors that determine in no small measure the way the adult world deals with the younger generation. It may be much healthier if adults admitted their hidden hostility toward the young and stopped pretending they are the benign and paternal guardian of their character and personality.

I think the betrayal of the young can better be seen if we look more specifically at persons and institutions in the adult world that deal with youth. If we ask young people how they feel about these problems, I think they would not have a feeling that they had been brutally treated or bitterly neglected, but that they had been trapped. It is not an unimportant description, for it is a term derived from the sport of hunting and means to capture a creature alive without physically harming for the purpose of domestication or the like. I think the young feel *caught* in a world they didn't make.

One trap for the young is the *love trap,* and the parents of children are the ones involved here—both the negligent ones who deprive the young of self-identity by loveless relationships and the well-meaning ones who surround the child with everything but direction and authority. We spoke before of our cheating the younger generation out of their rebellion, so necessary to maturity. Even in the delinquent subculture of today's youth, it is not true that the youngster is some "rebel without a cause" (this is Hollywood romantics). The boy and girl in trouble are not always rebelling against what their parents stand for; on the contrary, they may be acquiescing in the family values (or lack of them), expressing, if you will, the parents' own confused and in some cases immoral principles of behavior. The stereotype of the delinquent acting out a revolt against his family is many times far from the actual circumstances. I sometimes wondered as I sat in juvenile court and watched the parents while their kids were being sentenced by the judge—the sense of grief and bafflement, and in some cases embarrassment, of a mother and father when the kid is charged with some offense. They were embarrassed not because the child had strayed so far from their teachings and example, but because he mirrored them all too honestly.

The parents realized, perhaps only dimly, that there before
the judge's bench was their own self—*their* life, *their* principles, embodied not only in the child but in his delinquent act.

But even in the more normal, nondelinquent young, we find
the parents' betrayal indelibly marked upon their personalities.
We are facing now the first generation of *understood* children.
The understood child (and God knows he has almost as many
problems as the neglected one) has his own pathology that
stems from the lack of opportunity for rebellion against parents
who understood rather than gave him direction. The psychia-
trists are telling us of the vital importance of a strong father
image against which children can revolt. (Perhaps it is significant that the present generation grew up as children in a time
when most of their fathers were away at war.) As I look back
on my own life, I discern in retrospect how unconsciously
skillful my father was at providing that hard wall of parental
authority against which I could hammer out my youthful
rebellion—the young against the old, child against parent, that
protest which is as old as life itself. We need parents un-
threatened by and unfearful of their children, giving them
purpose with love, direction with affection, marking the limits
of their freedom within the atmosphere of unlimited acceptance of them as human beings.

Then there is the *school trap*—the persons involved in this
one are teachers, counselors, principals and administrators. It
is undoubtedly true that the "system" in large measure dictates
the attitudes of teachers and school personnel, but this does
not make the fact any less tragic that the school, in the same
way as the parents, fails the young and forsakes them at the
point of their greatest need. The school is prepared to make
good Americans (teachers and curriculum still operate on the
melting pot theory), skilled job finders, and socially adequate
youngsters; but in accomplishing this it fails the young at the

crucial point where they should be defining their experiences, appreciating diversity, valuing their individuality.

For example, teachers and schools have a gentle way of collaring and cutting off the self-propelled curiosity of youth. The really significant questions often are shunted aside as not being the task of the school or he is referred to some other compartment of life (for example, public issues and large political questions). And so the student learns subtly what questions not to ask. And again the deep need of the adolescent for self-respect is inevitably tied to social skills, adjustment and success. The teacher sees the student most of the time only as a problem in social integration and not as a human person growing to maturity and in special need of coming to respect himself.

This is particularly true of the youngster who comes from a lower socioeconomic class and is provoked into antisocial behavior by the middle-class expectations of the school he attends. When he fails to conform to these, he is treated as a social degenerate to be punished. The sad fact is that the schools seem no more capable today of handling the problem of authority than the parents, and there is no room in its tidy and well-ordered manipulativeness for the aberrant behavior or any completely individual response. Once again the young are trapped by the institutional snares of the adult world and tamed into mediocre domesticity. This is not a plea for acceptance of wildness and anarchic action by the young, but it is an appeal for genuine respect in the schools for those marvelous mutations of the human personality that occur now and again and that resist, sometimes violently, all efforts to smother with either understanding or punishment their integrity and independence.

The most important question facing older adults today as they deal with the young is: how can we give the young what we don't have? How can we bequeath a heritage not our own? The younger generation has come off better than any of us have a right to expect. Perhaps if we are penitent and seek out the young and give them direction and share our wisdom (not our knowledge), they will forgive us for our betrayal.

Technics and Teleology in American Life

THE "UGLY AMERICAN" and all other partially perverted images this nation projects into this world between the ages have been developed in large measure out of a heavy overemphasis on our technical superiority and good old American "know-how," without reference to goals and purposes that created and guided the destiny of our nation. The twentieth century has seen the growth in this country of one of the most advanced industrial and technological societies in the world. Only in recent decades has there been anything resembling a challenge to this scientific and social progress and that in the new world power of Russia. Even the most biased person must admit the fruits of material advancement are sweet indeed, and most of us have enjoyed those fruits even as we have been merciless critics of a growing technological society.

I grow weary of that incessant wailing, by our own critics, and by leaders of Asiatic thought, about the rampant scientism and materialism of American culture. The latter complain while making sure that as much of this tainted progress as possible is imported for their own consumption. I also resent the frequency of verbose tirades against the evils of technological advance as if our "know-how" were the only reason for humanity hurtling down a dead-end street at reckless speed. However, I think it very necessary that we examine rather carefully whether or not we are suffering from an obsession with technics or "know-how" to the exclusion of other considerations. This does not mean that we accept the superficial criticism of romantic thinkers who contrast the technical efficiency of the West with the alleged higher spirituality of the East; but it does mean, I believe, that the preoccupation in recent years with the building of an advanced technological society, together with the production and packaging of an American image of a sheer instrumentalist and highly developed technical society, has served to distort and denigrate the basic and fundamental values of our culture.

I think we must consider that in a society where we are obsessed with technique, whether it be how to get a hydrogen warhead into the middle of Moscow or build a better mousetrap or devise a machine to replace thinking, technical knowledge begins to assume a primacy even in relation to modes of thinking.

Can it be that we are so immersed in our own cultural assumption that we cannot see, for example, the utter instrumentalism of our society? Technical and functional questions predominate, and the larger meanings and ends of life are either obscured or falsified. We are notoriously inclined to emphasize the short run, the tangible and the quantitative.

William Lee Miller, a political writer for *The Reporter* magazine, was taking President Kennedy to task for his commencement address at Yale University in which he told the graduates that the really important questions before us now are not "political" or "questions of value" but largely "technical judgments." In putting into perspective the President's postulate, Mr. Miller makes this cogent point:

Where the end is simple and non-controversial such a technical problem raises no problems. But in social policy the ends to be served admit of no such description; it is of the essence of politics that their meanings shift, their values conflict and that men differ about them. The ends are not neatly separated from the "means" the technical man thinks he deals with exclusively; usually he bootlegs in some assumptions about ends in his work on the means.

When we are too committed to the technical, to practical and limited ends without larger ends and objectives, there is nothing to discipline, direct and criticize techniques. In a vacuum of goals and purposes, there is no reason why we should not spend billions on a shot to the moon instead of feeding the starving children of India or financing a continental "operation bootstrap" for all of Africa. Our obsession with *technical* reason (know-how) tends to underplay the *substantial* reason that deals with the ends and purposes to which our technics are directed. If we can imagine a community of men who know how to do everything but do not know that anything is worth doing, then nothing would be done and the human "know-how" would rust unused. It is probably therefore wrong to speak of a technical civilization—there are civilizations that use techniques in the service of their civilized purposes. It seems altogether possible that America could become a strictly utilitarian society not because we denied the validity of values and purposes—the teleology of our culture—but simply because we ignored them or made them subservient to technical mores.

There is a reductionism that accompanies technicism which presumes that the approach which may be appropriate for dealing with tangible problems, when the ends are limited and immediate, can also apply to *all* the problems of life. There is, for example, that terrifying next step in scientific advance beyond motivation research and depth psychology. At least one engineering journal and plenty of professors of biochemistry are talking about "custom-made man," built by the technique of human engineering to be the most cooperative and helpful kind of human being. When the biophysicist takes over with the technique of biocontrol, the mental processes, emotional responses and sense perceptions will be controlled by bioelectric signals; thus the right mental and emotional reaction can be created by electronics. How about that for prog-

ress? Can you imagine the comitragedy of a human short
circuit that causes you to laugh at Jesus being crucified and
makes you nauseated when you hear Beethoven's *Ninth
Symphony*?

The very techniques which helped bring about mass society
are the instruments of the destruction of man—man is treated
as a "hand," a machine, a robot, an impersonal thing. He is
regarded as something other than a human creature that thinks
and wills and feels. Mumford's analysis of our condition is
incisive.

Modern civilization has been arrested in midflight. Its technical
advances in saving labor, perfecting automatism, mechanizing the
daily processes of life, multiplying the arts of destruction, and de-
humanizing the personality have been responsible for this arrest.
The rise of the machine and the fall of man are two parts of the
same process. Never before have machines been so perfect and
never before have men sunk so low.

In the process of technocratizing we are likely to labor under
the illusion that not only will we be new kinds of men because
of techniques, but that all we need is *more* techniques. If we
can just lengthen the vision of our eyes so that we can see
unicellular life five hundred miles beneath the sea or just
increase our auditory capacity so we can hear a heartbeat on
another planet, then all will be well; but these are dubious
gifts without life and goals and purpose that are qualitatively
different. Without a significant place in our education and life
for the latter, we may be inhabitants of a world that is replete
with means but no meanings.

The temptations and danger marks are all around us. In
this time of great world crises, the opportunity for achieving
our historic purposes and exemplifying our characteristic values is great, but we may be easily deluded into spending all
our time, energy and talk on how to do more efficiently and
faster rather than on the knowledge of what to do. This pre-

occupation with technics, "know-how," is producing in our national life a new kind of philosophy and basic presuppositions that refuse to have anything to do with ultimate purpose and values. And on a less intellectual level, we are developing a new kind of popular culture and mass man, a man living on the surface of events, with his working life consumed in the service of technics and his leisure life distracted. His is a life deprived of the depth and meaning only purpose and values can give. So we see the "hollow men" of Eliot's poetry, who are estranged from the heart and substance of the tradition of civilization, that is, their heritage, who lead lives where "know-how" replaces "know-why," technics replace teleology, competence crowds out compassion, and technical reason invents its own new values of efficiency, output and production.

The tragedy of this preoccupation with technics is put in true perspective when we acknowledge the great ideological battle for men's minds and spirits which is part of the world scene today. The openness of the world to new leadership and the rise of underdeveloped nations make even more crucial the need to develop an American animus which we can put forth to the world as well as to remind ourselves. The nations of the world are aware of our technical and scientific advance; they have imported our "Coca-Cola culture," our tractors and trucks and new agriculture methods (they're also getting those from Russia and many of the products are equally good), but what they haven't got from us—because we haven't convinced ourselves that they are necessary—are the ultimate purpose and values for which our American life stands. This is why so much of the criticism of Americans by other nations is valid. They have a reason to wonder about the true nature of this country and where its leadership will take the world. We resent the gnawing doubts of the world about our capacity, but they are there. Nowhere are they more bluntly described than in

D. H. Lawrence's novel, *The Plumed Serpent,* in the thoughts
of Kate Leslie, the chief protagonist of the novel:

And sometimes she wondered whether America really was the great
death-continent, the great NO! to the European and Asiatic and
even African YES! Was it really the great melting pot where men
from creative continents were melted back again, not to a new
creation, but down into the homogeneity of death? Was it the great
continent of the undoing and all its peoples the agents of the mystic
destruction! Plucking, plucking at the created soul in a man, until
at last it plucked out the growing germ and left him a creature of
mechanism and automatic reaction, with only one inspiration, the
desire to pluck the quick out of every living spontaneous creature.
Was that the clue to America, she sometimes wondered? Was it
the great death-continent, the continent that destroyed again what
other continents had built up? The continent whose spirit of place
fought purely to pick the eyes out of the face of God. Was that
America?
    And all the people who went there, Europeans, Negroes, Jap-
anese, Chinese, all the colors and the races, were they the spent
people in whom the God impulse had collapsed so they crossed
to the great continent of the negation where the human will declares
itself "free" to pull down the soul of the world? Was it so? And did
this account for the great drift to the New World, the drift of spent
souls, passing over to the side of Godless democracy, energetic
negation? The negation which is the life-breath of naturalism. And
would the great negative pull of the Americans at last break the
heart of the world?

I don't know any place that the need for serious reflection
and articulation about our American purpose is more exposed
than in the slogan of today's "peacemongers": "I'd rather be
Red than dead." Any seriously intelligent person who is going
to challenge that "life-clutching" posture must come to grips
with American civilization and life at levels in which technical
and scientific progress have only the most peripheral meaning.
We must develop out of an internal dialogue a basic *raison
d'être* for our national existence and the life together we have
fashioned out of the conglomerate mass that makes up America;
what is called for is a solid affirmation of the basic ends to

which this nation is dedicated. We need a "new patriotism" to which men of all social and political loyalties can give some allegiance without shame or embarrassment.

As I see it, there are two major blocks to the development of such an affirmation of our way of life. First, there is the chauvinism and self-righteousness of the old nationalism of the Right; this is combined with the slick paper half-truths mouthed by a conservative and reactionary element to serve their own economic interests. The flag-waving, Fourth of July oratory, which tries to pass America off as God's special chosen nation to lead all other peoples out of darkness and whose shortcomings (if there are any) are balanced against our obvious superiority, proves finally to be the empty boastings of a guilty and insecure nation. The great French critic De Tocqueville discovered this American characteristic early in our history. In his *Democracy in America,* he reported:

If I say to an American that the country he lives in is a fine one, "Aye," he replies, there is not its equal in all the world. If I applaud the freedom which its inhabitants enjoy, he answers, "Freedom is a fine thing but few nations are worthy to enjoy it." If I remark on the purity of morals which distinguishes the United States, he declares, "I can imagine," says he, "that a stranger who has been struck by the corruption that prevails in other nations would be astonished at the difference." At length I leave him to a contemplation of himself. But he returns to the charge and does not desist until he got me to repeat all that I have been saying. It is impossible to conceive a more troublesome and garrulous patriotism.

And it persists to the present day. With the help of *Time* and *Life* (those deserving whipping boys of cultural criticism), this spiritual pride of our patriotic charlatanry can be seen and read daily and weekly in our media.

Also this old patriotism tended strongly to identify superiority with the very technics and "American know-how" we have been discussing. Its proponents somehow believed that inventiveness was more important than integrity, or that cleanliness was a substitute for godliness, or that speed made up for a lack of strength of purpose. They believed that the mountains of manufactured goods would be impressive enough to cover the emptiness of our spiritual values and purposes, which we won and lost the while. We learned our lesson the hard way in the ideological Cold War of the fifties when Russia came closer and closer to outproducing us and actually moved ahead in the rocket field. Our superiority was shaken in the scientific and technological fields (areas where we were certain Providence had given us unchallengeable primacy), so we turned frenetically toward trying to discover what we euphemistically called our national goals. One thing seems to be certain—the flag-waving, superpatriotic shibboleths that have passed for the basis of our loyalty and the core of our citizenship indoctrination are bankrupt, and the leaders of this nation in both political parties had better know it.

The second major obstacle to the building of a platform for a new patriotism is the hypercritical negativism and resultant paralysis of the intellectual Left in this country. I feel some confidence in what I have to say now because I have been and still am a part of that element, both as a friend of its essential philosophy and a sympathizer of the forms that its political rebellion has taken. I would like to make a distinction between the cerebral Left whose radicalism takes the form of social and political action and the emotional-psychological Left whose revolt is apolitical and takes the form of artistic-poetic disengagement from the current culture as evidenced in the nonconforming disaffiliates (who were once called "beats"). Now as for the former, it looks as though the politics of rebellion are dead, and we now have the politics of manipulation and adjustment. A great portion of the political Left made this choice when they became "chastened" or "realistic" liberals and were forced to choose between political philosophizing at the periphery or effectual action in the arena of party politics. Another contingent of the political Left refused to make the choice and instead took the vows of political chastity, choosing to espouse the doctrinaire slogans of their political past no matter how ineffective they were.

Now as to the lyrical, nonconformist Left, we had every right to hope that some kind of critical and careful reexamination might lead to a new affirmation of who we are as Americans, and what the purposes are that all our vaunted technics would serve. I, for one, have given up hope that politics (in any of its manifestations) will provide the fundamental breakthrough we need. A former associate of mine had this to say about the "beat movement," and I think he is right "that in its honest moments [it] arose in reaction to America's spiritual sickness. It arose as an on-the-road search for the lost American mystique, for the lost Whitmanesque capacity to wonder at the American earth and as a bitter rejection of the Moloch-mind which led us to barter our lyric possibilities for the bargains of commerce; it is a thumb nose put-down of an America that flirts with God and banks with Chase Manhattan." Now if this is true, this movement, assisted and accompanied by the avant-garde elements in the arts, has bogged down or gotten lost in the search so that it has ended up "howling" in the parochial wilderness of its own subjectivism or whimpering like a lost child that it's getting dark and the Bomb is going to fall and America is dead. But what about the search for the "American mystique"—the know-why—the values and purposes that make us believe (even after we have affirmed most of the beat critique) that our nature and destiny as a people have enough value to make us willing to sacrifice our lives for its survival?

It is my firm belief that if there is to be a new and dynamic affirmation of the basic value of this nation against all tyrannical totalitarianisms that threaten to do us in, it will have to come from the very Left that I have just been chastising.

Hopefully this will come before we succumb to a national despair and cynicism that could drive us into policies and decisions leading to our destruction.

In making this suggestion, it perhaps is my responsibility to put down some guidelines for a new patriotism. It of necessity cannot be full or final but simply hints at the direction. My desire to offer this grows out of my revolt against self-righteous and hypocritical political oratory and out of the weariness with American cultural criticism that seems impotent to develop any real basis for national loyalty.

First, the prerequisite for any such new affirmation is the confronting of the truth about ourselves as a people and the world in which we live. Keats coined the words:

> To bear all naked truths
> And to envisage circumstance, all calm
> That is the top of sovereignty.

This means that we will give up all illusions and delusions about this nation and its people, especially the one that we possess some kind of intrinsic superiority—only a tyranny can live by the lie. And this important fact is to be at all times before us, that "democracy professes less to possess the truth than to pursue it," and without the pursuit of it and the courage to face it we will suffocate. John Emmet Hughes, vouching for this veracity, speaks firmly to us in *America the Vincible:*

The People, who need love the rule of freedom enough to suffer the rigor of truth, seek first the faults in themselves. They scan their own speech for words that deceive. They scan their own history for legends that delude. They try to discern in their own conduct both excessive pretense of purpose and the insufficient force of practice.

Let us not be deceived though, for the pursuit and discovery of truth about ourselves will not make us free as those slogans over our science laboratories and halls of learning say. It may, to the contrary, bind us to the results of past action that we cannot redeem. Will Durant, the renowned historian of philosophy, says "that the greatest mistake in human history was the discovery of truth. It has not made us free except from delusions that comforted us and restraints that preserved us. It has not made us happy, for truth is not beautiful and did not deserve to be so passionately chased. As we look on it now we wonder why we hurried so to find it."

It is an honest observation, not given to argue truth's non-existence, but to destroy all illusions about what its discovery means. It is hard; it will not give us peace of heart, but the facing of it will help make Americans people of integrity, and nothing is needed quite so desperately as this throughout the whole world. Any new patriotism, any apology for the value and meaning of this American civilization against all the tyrannies that challenge it must begin with an honest admission of those bloody marks upon the historical pages of our national existence that give lie to all our pretensions to clean hands and pure innocence—the rape of the Indian nations and the subsequent degradation and humiliation of their people that led to those ghettos of the Plains known as alternate homelands; the shame of discrimination and segregation of the Negroes in which millions of people were treated as second-class citizens for a hundred years; and the many other injustices and oppressions that have been part of our official and unofficial policy and practice as people. Any claims to superiority of our way of life over any other system must be predicated on the honest confessions of our sins.

We are not allowed the handicap of the gross prefabrication and the false reconstruction of history so that the errors turn out to be right choices, and heroes turn out to be archvillains, and heroic sacrifices are declared vulgar betrayals.

Only totalitarian countries can rewrite history and name new inventors and discoverers. Russia has carried this pre-

fabricated historicity to its most absurd conclusions so that
even dead heroes like Stalin have to be dug up and desecrated
for the sake of new interpretations of history.

Or there is that concomitant form of whitewash found in
the education of West Germans today that leaves great gaps
and deadly silences in the recent history of their nation. No!
There must be a truth that judges our historical errors and
the evil of our collective misjudgments. The greatest immorality of American participation in the ill-fated Cuban invasion
was not that we chose wrong in being a party to the fiasco; it
is that our representative before the nations of the world had
to lie and pretend that the facts of history were different than
they were, in this instance, and as a result the great differen-
tiation between Cuba and Hungary was narrowed considerably
to our eternal discredit. Auden is right: "True democracy
begins with free confession of our sins." I think death might
be preferable to living in a world where there is no truth and
error, no sin and righteousness where people and nations
could admit no guilt or wrong—where slavery was really
freedom—and war was peace.

Part of the genius and distinctive value of our American
way and which we must always include as an integral part
of any patriotism is the openness and willingness to investigate
our faults and put our sins on record. Lord Bryce, the English
critic, said of Americans in *The American Commonwealth*,
"They know and are content that all the world should know
the worst as well as the best of themselves. They have a
boundless faith in free inquiry and full discussion. They admit the possibility of any number of temporary errors and
delusions." This posture is worth preserving against all political and national expediencies which would dictate its suspen-
sion in behalf of some larger good.

The love of one's country and culture, like the love of oneself, can come only after we have faced ourselves as we really are, known the misery and the grandeur, the perversity and the potential, the sickness and the health of our true condition. True love and reverence for our American forms of life can only come with such honesty—everything else is narcissistic infatuation, blind to all that makes us so unloving to others. In *This Bent World*, Langmead Casserly in discussing the difference between nationalism and patriotism claims that the latter is not an "ism" at all in the sense of having a developed ideology:

> The patriot does not love his country *because* . . . He simply loves his country, it is the place where he feels at home, where he finds and knows the people he understands, a place that belongs to him precisely because he belongs to it. The patriot sympathetically comprehends precisely why other people love the country to which they belong just as much as he loves his own. He doesn't need to romanticize or invent some pseudo-philosophy about the race to which he belongs. . . . True love is not called upon to justify itself by vindicating or white washing the beloved.

My basic dissatisfaction with the liberal and nonconformist critique of American and Western culture is not that it is critical and harsh with our faults but that it is grounded and impotent in its despair. I am weary of criticism and disparagement and the put-down that can't get up off its back. It is essential to condemn, but quickly, and then get on with the praise—of that which deserves praise. I am impatient with the sophisticated critic who finds little to choose from between Russian materialism and American materialism. Richard Hilary coined a phrase before he died in combat in World War II. He said, "We were fighting a lie in the name of a half-truth." It's a terrible dilemma, but no worse than many others we're asked to live with in this life. But let's get one thing straight. The innocence and naïvete have been shattered by the recorded events of our time. Camus put it clearly in *Resistance, Rebellion and Death,* when describing the experiences which had greatly influenced his work and thought. He said:

History progressed, East Berlin, Poznan, Budapest . . . A gigantic myth collapsed. A certain truth which had long been disguised burst upon the world. And if the present is still splattered with blood and the future still dark, at least we know that the era of ideologies is over, and the force of resistance, together with the value of freedom, gives us new reason for living.

These "new reasons" must be made incarnate in any basic affirmation or patriotism that we develop. The task is not simple, because we cannot easily turn shibboleths and slogans and worn-out words into dynamic tenets that we can nail to the door of every new despotism and say, "So help me God, here I stand!" Arthur Koestler in the epilogue to his recent comparative study of the culture of East and West, *The Lotus and the Robot,* holds up two great conclusive contributions that Western culture has made. They are "continuity in change" and "unity in diversity." Our American culture has a more important stake in these two contributions than the rest of the West, and they are greatly to be prized. One cannot understand this country, neither its history nor its nature, without tracing the role of these principles in its life.

Continuity in change is the value of preserving the very best of tradition and past without stifling the future and blinding ourselves to the vision that makes change and new ways a necessity. This may best be described in an imagery of our human vision and the way it operates. Men, having only two eyes, are forced to see in one direction—to see one thing clearly, it is necessary not to see something else at all. This is an optical law inherent in our human vision, and it is analogous to the limitations and finitude of the human psyche. This is why traditions and history (both knowledge of and reverence for them) are so important in preserving the balance in our culture. Tradition corrects the blindness of this present age by giving an account of how our forefathers saw things when looking in a different direction. Change gives tradition its vitality by adding vision of the future to vision of the past. God help us when we are unable to combine the new and the old into a single, life-giving vision!

The great value of this vision is that it prevents us from having to rewrite our history so that every past action, right or wrong, must be made submissive to contemporary thought. A completely *modern* society, with the past and tradition expurgated, always seems to produce a totalitarian culture with utopian illusions; history is one stumbling, bumbling host of errors to be forgotten and corrected by modernism. We have preserved the past, are respectful of its victories, regretful of its sins, and fearless of change. The Civil War, with its bloodshed and heartbreak and ugly scars on the human spirit too deep to heal, is ours to claim and acknowledge. John Brown's body is *our* body—everyone's and we dare not deny it.

The second theme, *unity in diversity,* is at the heart and soul of the American experiment. As never before, we must lift this up as the inner core of our faith. Our *unity* never has been, is not now, and never will be *uniformity.* So clear and strong is this principle that there probably can never be a single "mystique" which is American, no "Zeitgeist" which sums up what we are and stand for. Even our goals and purpose will not be a single list to which we all give assent, nor will there be a single political or national orthodoxy by which the faithfulness of citizens is measured. For our unity is in the diversity of peoples, faiths, philosophies which make up this country. And the extent to which we protect it by law and in the spirit, that *diversity* will be the measure of our real respect for our way of life. There is built into the American makeup (and it has sprung out of the religious and secular faiths that fed America) the belief that every point of view has great value. There is no voice or view so insignificant or so troublesome that it should be stamped out. The singularity of a solidarity to which all opposing voices are sacrificed is foreign to us, and the price we pay is a sacrifice of total agreement, a seeming divisiveness.

This great principle is nourished by the spirit of liberty which all of us profess but few of us practice—the spirit that Justice Learned Hand spoke of in his essays *The Spirit and Liberty*:

The spirit of liberty is the spirit that is not too sure it is right; the spirit of liberty is the spirit which seeks to understand the minds of other men and women; the spirit of liberty is the spirit which weighs their interest alongside its own without bias; the spirit of liberty remembers that not even a sparrow falls to earth unheeded. . . .

If you tell me that this is too uncertain and displays a weakness unbecoming a person or a nation confident of why it is here and what its destiny is, I can only say that it is not so. This is our strength. The critic of American softness and confusion of goals, who claims the Communist will win the ideological Cold War and any hot war because he knows exactly what he wants, tells me nothing about the superiority of Communism over our democracy; he simply is reciting the fighting advantage of an unquestioning and absolute fanaticism.

The spirit of liberty may not always make us united in policy; we may sometimes appear weak and divided. It will not always make us first in war, but it will ultimately triumph because it is eternally right. Our strength does not lie in any conviction that beyond all doubt we are right and the rest of the world is wrong, but in the belief that all men and nations together in diversity contribute to the unity of humankind. This spirit cannot flourish in any totalitarian system, whether

Fascist or Communist or any new versions. I do not relish living where that spirit is suffocated and destroyed on behalf of some false promise of a greater freedom or a better life or a larger truth. Each element and event in our national life that mocks *this spirit* impoverishes us and disqualifies our every claim to moral leadership in the world. The spirit is gentle and fragile, and we must nurture it with great care. Amid the uproar and clash of nations and ideas, it seems to have been suppressed and trampled, but I believe it will live.

Finally, at the base of all that America claims to be, and now and again exemplifies, is the respect and value it places on individual man, that recalcitrant, unadjusted, unpredictable spirit that is the human person. This is why there are volumes of essays and books on the depersonalization and degradation of man in contemporary society. Deep down we believe that no manipulation of the masses, no artificial insemination of communal conformity, no means of governing or ways of pressuring which dehumanize and degrade the human spirit are ever justified. And here is our real danger in America, not from the Left that would betray us or from the Right that would make us unholy crusaders but from the Middle that would allow our lives subtly to be automatized and our senses brutalized. We must resist this with all our hearts. This land will be a freer place every time you love without calculating a return, every time you make your drudgeries and routines still more inefficient by stopping to experience the shock of beauty wherever it flickers, every time you assert your stubborn spirit when you feel the pressures of social conformity squeezing the will to resist out of you. Vachel Lindsay said, "Change not the mass but change the fabric of your own soul and your own visions and you change all." We must learn well the goal of all collectivist machines and totalitarian systems—it is the *disincarnation of man.*

Everyone who really loves this country must help project, for the sake of ourselves and others, the fundamental purposes and goals toward which our nation moves, and hopefully all our inventiveness, scientific ingenuity and technics may serve those ends which we cherish and which, in the long run, are the only things worth sacrifice.

The Dialogue of Democracy

ONE OF THE MOST unique and thoroughly American cultural phenomena is our *modus operandi* for peaceful coexistence between divergent ethnic and religious elements in our society. The system developed in our country is pluralism, a cultural situation whereby no one religious or ideological point of view is the national one, and any attempt to put one religious view above any others always runs up against intense public opinion and reaction. American unity is not achieved by a single purpose or point of view; therefore our unity is not monolithic but pluralistic. Now this has not meant that the state did not believe religion was a basic human concern; as a matter of fact, it has assumed responsibility for protecting religious liberty along with all other liberties. It is true, too, that American pluralism, for the most part, is religious by nature; and, while many people believe that this "way of life" released much energy and was a creative force in our country, one would also have to admit that this pluralism has created historic tensions, group rivalry and conflict over constitutional principles. It is important if we are to understand this dialectical nature of our democracy to look at the historical roots of this concept.

Reinhold Niebuhr traces the origins of democracy in the Anglo-Saxon world to the multiplication of Puritan sects in the Cromwellian period of the seventeenth century, because these sects challenged the monarchy as unjust and the established church of Tudor England as invalid. Out of the Crom-

[85]

wellian revolt, though it didn't last long, came two basic ideas: 1) the supremacy of Parliament and 2) a pluralistic society in which unity could be achieved by toleration of different religious views. Niebuhr claims that "The spirit of toleration is an absolute necessity for any pluralistic society, for unless men understand the possibility of error lurking in *their* truth and are prepared to glean some truth in the errors which they combat there is no possibility of that 'limited warfare' which is rightly the basis of democratic society."

This conflict and tension are inevitable in a society of multiple faiths, and we will discuss later the nature of this warfare and how it contributes to justice in the balancing of interests. Father John Courtney Murray claims that we do not have to probe deeply beneath the surface of civic amity to uncover the structure of passion and war. There is the underlying resentment of the Jew so long dependent on the acceptance and goodwill of a Christian community that all too often lighted the fires of anti-Semitism with basic misunderstanding. There is the profound distrust of Catholics and Protestants of each other. Catholics remember Cromwell's crusades, the Know-Nothing nativism of nineteenth-century America, and even the presidential election of 1960. The Protestants remember Inquisition in ancient Spain and persecution in modern Spain, and the political domination in lands where the Catholics are a majority.

All of these memories are part of our attitudes toward the different religions in our culture, and no amount of sweet talk about reasonableness and common aims will serve to hide the war that goes on between these groups. Despite the past, however, the problems resulting from American pluralism have been fought out largely in the courtrooms and school boards of this nation, rather than in bitterness and violence of open group conflict. There are of course historical exceptions to the peaceful approach. When one remembers, for example, that it was less than one hundred years ago in Philadelphia that the homes of Roman Catholic citizens were burned and there were pitched battles in the streets of the city, the dissonant noise of school boards bickering seems mild in comparison and looks like real progress.

As a result of the battle being confined to legal principles, there has developed on the question of separation of church and state and religious liberty, if not a single agreement, at least a posture of pluralism that finds normative for America "free religion in a free society"—that is no religion under the coercion or interference of the state, and no state under the coercion or interference of religion. It is generally agreed that the First Amendment of the Constitution means there may be *no religious establishment* in this country, even if there are differences on how much aid may be given to any religious group in encouragement or support.

Equally as important, however, as the historical and legal heritage of our pluralism is the sociological transition that has taken place in the United States since its founding. In this transition are the seeds of destruction of our pluralistic culture, and this sociological analysis might be called the Herberg thesis growing out of Will Herberg's *Protestant, Catholic, Jew.* In this book he traces the development of the tripartite religious pluralism of democratic America. It is Herberg's concept that in the past generation we have grown from a Protestant nation into a three-religion country, and that whereas originally one's identity as an American came from the immigrant cultural or ethnic group, today, it is presumed the religious implication of being an American is that one is either a Catholic, Protestant or Jew. This is so firmly fixed that when we talk about pluralism in America we are talking about *religious pluralism.* There are at least two important ways of looking at this pluralism: on one level these three religious groups are cultural subcommunities defining three different ways of being

American; on another level, however, they are three different religious systems with beliefs, liturgies and institutions.

In his book, Herberg spoke about the Kennedy study in the early 1940's of intermarriage trends in New Haven, Connecticut, from 1870–1940. In the publication of her findings, Ruby Jo Reenes Kennedy points out that "Future cleavage . . . will therefore be along religious lines rather than along nationality lines as in the past. Cultural lines may fade but religious barriers are holding fast. . . . The traditional single melting pot idea must be abandoned and a new conception, which we term 'the triple melting pot theory' of American assimilation will take its place. . . . The different nationalities are merging but within three religious compartments rather than indiscriminately." Her findings seem to have been borne out sociologically as the religious community has emerged as the prime factor of self-identity and social focus in contemporary American life.

However, Herberg went a step further to point up a fourth religious development which may prove yet to be the greatest threat to pluralism. This is what he calls "civic" or "culture" religion. John Courtney Murray, in his essay *Four American Conspiracies*, identifies this fourth religion as secular humanism. This fourth religion has been called America's religion, but, though it seems to combine the three traditional faiths, it is not a synthesis of the beliefs found in these religions. Eugene Carson Blake has described it thus:

This ideology is what an American is if nobody tampers with his attitudes. His articles of faith are science (its engineering application), common sense (his own ideas), the Golden Rule (its negative form), sportsmanship and independence. I have called this humanism not because he doesn't believe in God. He does, but his god is not to be confused with a transcendent being to whom he owes duty and life itself but rather his god is a combination of whipping boy, servant and useful ally.

The dominance of this "faith" hardly needs to be documented since its adherents daily pound our ears with its shibboleths and theology, and the traditional faiths are subsumed under the rubric of "interfaith" or the American way. Arthur Mann of Massachusetts Institute of Technology, writing in *Commentary*, says:

What the Deists hoped to achieve without a church has in large degree come to pass in the land of many churches. Indeed this idea that religion is a handmaiden to democracy has made such headway that American Catholicism, American Protestantism, and American Judaism appear like parallel shoots in a common stock.

And so the democratic faith becomes the ultimate religion in this country. Before this "humanistic nationalism," the three traditional religions appear provincial and divisive and point up the diversity among us, while the religion of the American way is the great unifying force and faith in this country. I think Herberg is right in his thesis about the tripartite division which serves to identify persons, but the religion that seems to be all inclusive is to be an American. This "common faith" has had a remarkable influence upon Catholicism, Judaism, and Protestantism in this country and has Americanized these religions considerably.

It is my conviction that this "civic religion," while certainly not something to be feared, has a serious and enervating effect upon the American pattern of religious pluralism. I would suggest that there are several limitations and inherent dangers in the growth and influence of this fourth religion of America.

First, the preeminence of this democratic religion has the effect of devitalizing the historic faiths by blurring the distinctive contributions of each. If the dialogue of religious pluralism has had any power, it is in the honest respect for differences in faith and belief that characterize each religious group. Under the impact of a national faith such "differences" become un-American, and it is certainly not in the best national interest to highlight these important divergencies. This nationalized and religionized togetherness is not a substitute for the depth and vitality that historic Judaism and Christianity have contributed to American life. As one critic puts it:

Simple chumminess, whether imposed by national compulsion or generated by amiable syncretism, if it asks the price of commitment to truth as ticket to the arcades and temples of national religion, is dangerous.

Secondly, there is the inherent danger in the "fourth faith" of what Jacques Maritain calls the temporalization of religion. One of the best illustrations of how this happens is seen in the rather blatant way in which religion (particularly in the decade of the religious revival) was called on constantly to undergird and support the political policies of this country. Truman mouthed inanities about our foreign policy being based on the Sermon on the Mount, and John Foster Dulles spoke of the "moral foundations of our cold war postures." From "In God We Trust" on coins to the perfunctory prayers of official functions, we use religion (anybody's) to bolster the temporal order. Maritain says in his *Reflections on America:*

Just as it is not particularly favorable, as a rule, for religion to be too much brandished about and made use of by the officials of any government, so the much deeper phenomenon—temporalized religious inspiration in a nation or civilization—however normal and salutary it may be in itself, involves its own accidental dangers. The risk is that religion itself might become temporalized, in other words so institutionalized in the temporal structures themselves . . . that it would lose its essential supernatural, supra-temporal and supra-national transcendence and became subservient to particular national or temporal interests.

This phenomenon in recent decades has been all too apparent, for example, in the way in which religion was used in the service of national socialism in Germany and in fascism in Italy and Spain. But one may reply these were dictatorships and their religions were folk religions of race and soil, while here in America ours is a "democratic faith." I am not relieved by that assurance, for the tyranny of the majority, especially when buttressed by a religious aura, is just as dangerous as any totalitarianism. If religion is not in some measure transcendent over the temporal order, then it becomes subservient to that order.

Thirdly, the predominance of the "fourth religion" promises us the very real possibility that pluralism is being undercut by a new establishment of religion. The historic faiths will serve the American people best if they reject and protest this official sanctioning of democratic religion even if it seems to favor and conserve common values which we all claim. The establishment of this new religion will be much easier to attain because it promises to be no religion, but its myths are already immortalized in our history books; its secular creeds are the slogans of Americanism, with which every schoolchild is indoctrinated; its holy days are already state and national celebrations; its saints and martyrs are the heroes of our history.

Professor J. Paul Williams is the most dedicated supporter of the establishment of the new religion. In his book, *What Americans Believe and How They Worship,* he calls for Americans to look on the democratic ideal "as the will of God or if they please the Law of nature . . . democracy must become an object of religious dedication." In other words there is more than one way of subverting the American principle of separation of church and state—the nationalization of religion may be more of a threat than parochial schools. It was very telling, for example, how much of the vehement protest against the recent Supreme Court decision on the New York Board of Regents prayer came from people who were not committed members of Jewish or Christian communities, but were the adherents of "civic religion" which was undercut in its primary role of providing a foundation for our democratic process. Many of the true believers in American "secular faith" clamored that the Supreme Court had hastened the secularization of this nation (*sic!*).

What we have been saying here is that authentic pluralism as a way of living in unity with great diversity is the pattern which promises the most significant dialogue of understanding without surrendering the validity of the faith for which we live and may be willing to die. I am suspicious of all universal ideologies which profess to embrace all in a flabby tolerance that allows for no divergence of views; such religion always has a way of creating superficial harmony and a false unity that does not exist. Our need now *is the emphasis on diversity and not unity.* Pluralism, to be sure, has its dangers and limitations, but they are much less than the dangers of a unified, national faith. Pluralism has several important antecedents that must be recognized. When we talk about pluralism in this nation, we are not only referring to the allowance made for various versions of the Christian and Jewish faiths but also to the fair play given to the secular protest against religion. In cultures where there is no room for secular criticism, historic religions become static and reactionary.

Also pluralism requires a high degree of mutual toleration of the other's right to hold the faith that he wishes and to practice it within the limitations of other people's freedoms. Mutual respect and regard for the other person's religious liberty is a prerequisite to disagreement. The test of pluralism is our ability to work out in living relationships something resembling tolerable justice in areas of divergent interests and claims. There are several misconceptions under which pluralists labor.

First, they should have no illusions that the contributions of Judaism, Protestantism and Catholicism are the same—they are not. These historic faiths have brought a variety of emphases to the social and political scene of our country. Judaism's greatest contribution, I think, is its great *sense of justice* and the promotion of the general welfare. Its great prophetic tradition has instilled in our society an appreciation for the plight of the social underdog in our world. The Protestants (though possessing great diversity) have given us the *principle of protest and dissent* by which every absolute claim and truth is called into question. The Catholic Church has brought to our culture the emphasis on *permanence and order,* an order by which we can check the tyranny of license posing as freedom. All of these contributions are very different but very significant ones, and I for one would not like to be without any of them.

Another misconception that we suffer from is that each of these historical faith movements is a monolithic structure; but this is not realistic, for within each of these religious movements are individuals and groups with varying aspirations who live with serious tensions between their own way of life and the faith to which they belong. But we who are used to oversimplifying have thought that each group possessed its own uniformity. Most Protestants, and Baptists particularly, had already fitted Jack Kennedy into his rigid ideological armor of Roman Catholicism before he even spoke in the last presidential campaign. Many Baptists believed he took his orders from the Bishops and couldn't violate their edicts. How surprised they were at the open difference in the Catholic Church on federal aid to education with the President sounding more Protestant than some of their clergy. The Baptists might not have been so positive about Kennedy had they not such a short memory—it was one of their Presidents who appointed an envoy to the Vatican!

The tensions that have grown up in our pluralistic culture have been marked by misconceptions and misunderstandings, but more than that, the tensions do revolve around substantive

matters involving different beliefs. Just to enumerate some of
these practical disagreements: the feeling among some Catholics that they have a right to public support for their parochial
schools; the effort of both Roman Catholic and Protestant agencies to review and censor films and books in the interest of
public morality; the desire of many communities to display
Christian symbols on public tax-supported property or to intro-
duce Bible reading in the public schools; the effort of Jewish
organizations to effect liberalization of Sunday blue laws which
they feel discriminate against Jewish sabbatarians.

These tensions and conflicts which have grown up in communities all over America are important for the public dialogue
and understanding. The difficulty is that they are not faced on
the level of discourse and conversations between peoples. They
are either dealt with in the courts (which generally leaves
everyone as confused as before) or by a political power move
behind the scenes. It is my conviction that these tensions can
only be dealt with and genuine pluralism maintained only if
dialogue and the law are the instruments for religious expression.

At the risk of being misunderstood I must say that we
probably have gone far enough in the legal field for the moment and ought to hold off until community and public dialogue on the subject catches up with our legal decisions. Every
faith must be willing and able to hold conversations and open
discussions that deal with matters affecting public policy—such
as birth control, censorship, school issues. Much misunderstanding could be avoided if these matters were the subject of wide-
spread public discourse. All too often they are only talked
about in hushed tones by ecclesiastics of the same faith, and
the cross-fertilization of ideas never takes place; or they are the
subject of purely legal conversations having to do with law
and tradition and not with present realities. We will not avoid
serious clashes and conflicts, ill will and misunderstanding if

any group uses sheer political power to enforce its will without prior consultation with men of goodwill in every faith.

To illustrate: in the summer of 1958 in New York City, the Commissioner of Hospitals, himself a Jew, incurred the wrath of the Protestant Council, several Jewish groups, and a number of civil libertarian organizations because he would not authorize doctors who were treating city patients in these hospitals to prescribe contraceptive devices. The ban extended to non-Catholic patients treated by non-Catholic physicians. Catholics vigorously opposed lifting the ban because they believed that these practices were sinful; and, since hospitals were supported out of tax revenues, Catholic citizens should not pay for public services that are morally repugnant to them. The charge was freely made that the Archbishop of New York had put political pressure on the city administration. Robert F. Wagner, New York's Catholic mayor, "passed the buck" to the unhappy Commissioner of Hospitals.

All religious faiths will do the cause of religious freedom irreparable harm if they insist on pressing *their* claims only by private pressure and legal tactics, thus threatening the clarity of public debate, the process by which democratic political decisions are made, and the only means by which they may be rationally discussed and judged.

Lastly I want to discuss the future of religious pluralism and perhaps hint at the forms religious tensions may take in the future. First, I think that the *"limited warfare"* principle is necessary in a pluralistic culture. We will have to plan for the conflicts which are apt to occur when divergent faiths present their claims in an open society. We will not suppress our differences but value them. It is important to limit the warfare—the battle between religious groups must not become a deadly and pernicious struggle whereby we kill each other off, but a balancing of the rights and privileges of each group. The object in this warfare is not complete annihilation or unconditional surrender, but a balancing of claims and interests. We must not yield to the bigots and "know-nothings" who would push us into "all-out war," but on the other hand neither should we heed the admonitions of "interfaith cooperators" or "positive thinkers" who cry, "peace, peace" when there is no peace.

We must not put down every argument on public policy between Catholics and Protestants or between Christians and Jews as religious squabbling or sectarian divisiveness—it may be the necessary prelude to a just and durable compromise between conflicting interests.

The debate must be dignified, but it must go on; the warfare must be limited, but it must rage on above the spurious protest that all such controversy is a detriment to our national unity. I like Arthur Cohen's words on this subject:

Not only the religious community but the free society itself may succumb to absolutistic pretensions. It may do so by assuming that freedom consists in reaching agreement and absolute social harmony. To confuse freedom with consensus, to assume that the free society is one where no disagreement should exist is like saying if the pulse is even, low and unexciting the patient is healthy. It may be, rather, that the patient is just about dead.

The health and vitality of our three religious communities in America may be determined by the way in which we do battle in the common social and political order. There are hopeful indications that we may be moving out of the interfaith ethos with its suppression of diversity into an era of more forthright and honest debate of differences. Because not too long ago we all experienced what it was like to be a disfranchised minority, we are still a little defensive, so that it will be some time before Jews stop trying to censor *The Merchant of Venice* or can help feeling that Christmas trees are secret symbols of Christian anti-Semitism; or before Protestants stop protesting *Elmer Gantry* or believing that the repeal of Prohibition was a Catholic conspiracy of some kind; or before Catholics stop believing that every Protestant is a P.O.A.U. spy who thinks all Catholics are "foreigners and aliens."

The sooner we lay the old ghosts to rest the better it will be, but we must not listen to those who tell us that all the conflict is over. We must be prepared to live with a kind of "limited warfare" among diverse faiths in this country for some time to come. This warfare will be interrupted by numerous meetings at the peace table of discourse and understanding where each group is able to interpret its actions and the theological motivation for these actions. There must be no differences so deep and no ideas so divisive that meetings around this table seem utterly hopeless or impossible.

At the same time we accept the above admonition, we must be prepared to find means of *deepening the dialogue*. The various religious faiths must go into their public dialogue much further than interfaith seders, brotherhood weeks and weekend retreats to discuss our common heritage. In the future it won't be enough for rabbis and ministers to exchange pulpits or a priest to speak of the social vision of papal encyclicals. Clergy and laymen are going to have to stand up on the basic theological presuppositions of their own faith and confront their opponent with complete honesty and as much clarity as can be mustered. It will probably be necessary for more informed and articulate persons to enter the dialogue, those who are not willing to water down the essence of their faith so that it will be more palatable to their opponent.

Out of this more honest and straightforward posture will not necessarily come more "togetherness" between the historic faiths. The airing of our differences in this fashion could, for example, make clear that the cleavages that separate us are greater than we thought. Robert McAfee Brown, in *An American Dialogue*, comments on this:

The Protestant who naively hopes that Catholics will give up certain beliefs (such as the infallibility of the Pope) for the sake of unity is in for a depressing experience. The Catholic who hopes that Protestants can be brought back into Catholicism by the concession of some fringe benefits such as married clergy or permission to sing Wesley's hymns during mass is going to discover that Protestant convictions run deeper than that.

But this is the risk of deepening the dialogue, and we can't be content with a few interfaith meetings once a year—we must broaden the dialogue to include more people.

The Missing Dimensions in Politics

NO AREA of our public life has been so affected by the cata-
clysmic revolution of this world between the ages as the world
of politics. Industrialization, urbanization, war have all influenced our political life as a people. The rapid and radical
changes of these past decades have far outstripped the development of a political machinery commensurate with the
new world we are facing. Our political structures seem utterly
inadequate to cope with the new ways of living and the organization of our social life. The result of this "political lag" in
American life may be seen in the problems we face as a
people trying to participate in public decisions. There is no
area of our social existence where individuality seems to be
so out of fashion and impotent to deal with the great impersonal decisions of our collective life as it does in politics.

I recall James Wechsler's account in his book *Reflections
of an Angry, Middle-Aged Editor* of a symposium at Hunter
College in which he appeared with that "gone" celebrity of
the beat generation, Jack Kerouac. He described the SRO audience that jammed the auditorium at Hunter. It was the largest
audience of the young he had seen since the heyday of the
thirties—a majority being from late high school through college age—alive, vibrant, anticipatory. It seemed that they
were indulging the middle-aged member of the panel; they
were really there to catch the pearls of wisdom that fell from
the lips of Kerouac. Wechsler's comment on the beat generation was this:

[99]

The ranks of the beat are limited and scattered. It is hardly likely that what they are up to would evoke so much notice if most of their contemporaries were engaged in great exercises; what gives them part of their prominence—as it did "the lost" of the 1920's and the radicals of the 30's — is that they almost alone seemed to care very deeply, even if it was about the cult of not caring.

After speaking of this meeting at Hunter College, Wechsler compares it with a meeting a few weeks later at the Commodore, an informal session of leaders of the Americans for Democratic Action gathered to discuss the future of that organization. The youngest man in that meeting was Arthur Schlesinger, Jr., who had just passed his 40th birthday, and there was not among them a single person representing the generation born between 1925 and 1935.

I recall this incident from Wechsler's writings because it points up all too clearly one of the major dilemmas of politics in this country. It is becoming increasingly clear that we are suffering from the political disaffiliation of the young. Had it not been for Adlai Stevenson in the national campaigns of 1952 and 1956, the disengagement of the younger generation from active political life of this nation would have been even greater. There have been many analyses to explain this "disaffiliation," and they have run the gamut from the psychoanalysis of the "silent generation" to the terrible complexity of the international situation. These explications of the social sources of political irresponsibility may account in part for our present dilemma, but I would like for you to look into the political life of our country (or if this is too broad, just the political life of your own neighborhood) for the sources and reasons for our difficulty. It is the politicians, both professional and amateur; the party man and the "independent"; the pundits and critics of the political process who are in large measure responsible for the vacuum in the active political life of our nation. It is these people who have created the misshapen image of politics which the younger generation sees through and against which it revolts.

POLITICS AND POKER

In the Broadway musical, *Fiorello,* there was a smoke-filled backroom scene in which a group of political hacks were trying to find an opponent for the incumbent, and they sang a very humorous but cynical song about whom they could run. It reflected the deep-seated cynicism and distrust of politicians which date all the way back to Machiavelli. Politics is viewed as a vocation only a little higher than thievery. This is reflected in the comment of the editor of a liberal weekly that the last administration replaced Jefferson on three-cent stamps with the Statue of Liberty and the motto "In God We Trust" which seemed appropriate because there was no one else we could trust in the 69 square miles of the District of Columbia; or it is seen in the sneering comment of a politico, "Let me make the deals and I care not who makes the ideals." The misanthropic view of politics seems to be validated continuously in the history of all political parties in this country. The view suggests that politics is mainly a game of individual skills in skulduggery where greedy and power-lustful men divide up the loot after having cheated the public out of its rightful inheritance.

This cynical attitude has been fostered by the "boss image," the corrupt political machines of our large cities and in national conventions. It is important to realize that this view of politics is not just an "image," but partially in political reality a way of approaching politics, or manipulating processes and people for completely self-serving ends, of seeing politics as completely amoral without relationship to any prior value or ethical goals. What is significant is the corroding and debilitating effect this picture of political life as a phony, unauthentic existence has on the American public and the younger generation. Recently, I met a young man who is a governor's assistant; he had been a Protestant minister, and I asked him why he left the ministry. He said in effect that when he stood up on Sunday and lied about things he felt hypocritical, so he thought it better to be in a profession where lying was expected.

One cannot measure the influence that the pessimistic posture of politicians has had upon people who disengage themselves from a political process, which promises no hope that somehow politics might be wedded with integrity to the great unsolved problems of justice and freedom in our society. Our people need the assurance, beyond mere political rhetoric, that politics is not merely a backroom game where greedy men divide up the spoils of victory, but that political clubs, wherever they meet, are deeply concerned about the community and neighborhood they represent and *all* the human beings that make it up.

POLITICS AND PURISTS

The people who have done most to expose and help destroy the cynical view of politics in American life are the reformers. They have lived in every political age, and our own has its special breed of reformers. From these people comes new hope for political parties and the whole process by which we make our decisions in this country. In New York City, the reform movement in the Democratic Party has been a source of such hope, and new blood has been pumped into the Democratic Party in New York because this growing reform movement broadened the base of grass roots participation and took its message to the people. However, as reformers move close to power and control, they, too, are subject to the same temptations and become a source of disillusionment to the people. There are two such temptations and postures reformers sometimes fall into unwittingly but never without damaging people's faith in the political process.

First, is the difficulty with which reformers move from the

role of "outsiders" to that of responsible wielders of political
power. The struggle to gain influence and control the battle is
much like guerrilla warfare—the tactics are hard-hitting, the
forces undisciplined, the strategy diversified—but in a growing army and with victory near, there becomes a need for
disciplined troops and common strategy, and reformers are
often ill-prepared.

Part of the problem of this transition is for aspiring political
leaders to move from the abstraction of generality (and most
campaigns are won on this) to the concreteness of particularity.
It is an everlasting temptation for the reformer to stand
perched on the top of some Sinai, hurling down his principles
and positions for all men to affirm and put into practice.
However, when reformers engage in social and political action
at the level of neighborhood needs, they sometimes fail. For it
is on the neighborhood scene that our politics and good in-
tentions become irrelevant in the light of the local issues and
problems that confront us. When we move from the high-
sounding platforms of campaign oratory to the streets of Chicago's North Side, or Frisco's waterfront area, or New York's
Greenwich Village, we discover a confusion and complexity
about issues that we never counted on. There is nothing better
designed to send the enthusiastic reformer running back to
his books of Stevenson's speeches and summit meetings on
the future of liberalism than to encounter firsthand the ambi-
guities of a neighborhood issue. Often reformers beat hasty
retreats to the political club, there to discuss in unending
fashion phony procedural questions or the strategy of infighting
for the next battle in the reform movement.

The second danger of the reformer in the political arena is
that being a purist at heart he dons the uniform of the crusader, and, armed with a whole mess of morality and self-
righteous indignation, he is off to his holy war. His enemies
are *all* the opponents of his political purity, whether in- or

outside the reform movement. There the reformer often takes concrete political issues in which there is honest difference and invests them with a moral color and a highly emotional charge. The political purist needs to understand that politics is a matter of adapting oneself to all sorts of people and situations, a game in which one may score but only by accepting the rules and recognizing one's opponents, rather than a moral crusade in which one's stainless standard must mow the enemy down. If he does not understand this, he will finally destroy the movement which is the means of his reform. It is a fact of political history and experience that reform movements die of two causes—*relaxation*, the apathy which follows victory, and *internecine struggle* in which political convictions become like theological orthodoxy in the Church and only the "true believer" is allowed to survive. The atmosphere of political inquisitions is bitter and recriminatory and finally self-destructive. The reformer in order to avoid this fate must resist the temptation to be a *crusader*, and he must never believe, uncritically, his own campaign oratory. As many people are repulsed by the purity of political Pharisees as they are by the self-aggrandizement of cynical politicians.

PSEUDO-POLITICS

Another significant factor in the disaffiliation of this generation from political activity is due to something that has happened to us as a people. I want to refer to the thesis of Daniel Boorstin in his book *The Image* in which he claims that because we have nourished and harbored extravagant expectations for our nation and our lives, we created the demand for illusions with which we can deceive ourselves. The making of these illusions has become big business in America, and we have become so accustomed to our illusions that we mistake them for reality. One of the ways in which we satisfy our insatiable hunger for images is the creation of "pseudo-events" which are not spontaneous but preconceived, planted and incited. This is part of what Boorstin calls the Graphic Revolution which enables us to preserve, make, transmit and disseminate precise images of men, events, and landscapes at an unbelievable rate.

It is amazing how much we hear about, read about and look at pseudo-events until we finally believe they are reality. To illustrate the subtlety of this matter, last year in Times Square there was a peace demonstration that culminated in purported acts of police brutality and arrests. The lawyers signed up "eyewitnesses" to the happening only to find out that many of those who claimed they were eyewitnesses saw the event on television. Sooner or later we are unable to distinguish between "psuedo-events" and spontaneous happenings, between images and reality.

There are increasing numbers of people who know this is happening to us, and the political processes have suffered mightily from this phenomenon of our time. Politics becomes a succession of psuedo-events: fake press conferences created for effect on constituency, the "news leak"—an elaborately planned way of emitting information. We elect Presidents on the basis of their ability to appear well on television debates or interview shows. The political convention is the psuedo-political event par excellence. The sham and pretense, the drummed-up enthusiasm, the phony drama of wheels and deals —all are part of the manufactured *event*.

Nothing appears real or spontaneous in the political arena. Speeches are written by ghost-writers, memorized and passed out prior to the taped appearance on a prearranged interview. The questions are planned and the answers are canned. People begin to lose confidence that words mean anything, that speeches are for public consumption; press conferences are for public relations, not information—nothing "is for real." The political world has a cardboard stage.

POLITICS AND THE DOCTRINAIRE

Another factor in the alienation and disaffiliation of people from the world of politics is related to the fact that we do live in a postideological world, a world where ideology—whether leftist, rightist, existentialist or positivist—is dead. Daniel Bell in his book *The End of Ideology* deals with this revolution in thought in action. At one point in discussing the plight of the present generation he says:

> The problem for this generation . . . is the inability to define an enemy. One can have causes and passions only when one knows against whom to fight. The writers of the twenties scorned bourgeois mores. The radicals of the thirties fought "capitalism" and later fascism, and for some, Stalinism. Today, intellectually, emotionally, who is the enemy one can fight? . . . This is the end of an age. For the younger generation, as for all intellectuals, there is this impasse. It is a part of the time which has seen the end of ideology.

This fact I believe has serious implications for the political life of our country. Let's illustrate this problem. It used to be quite simple to identify a "liberal" in politics just by asking him where he stood on McCarthy, or civil rights or labor legislation, but in a political milieu where dogmatism is dead, "liberalism" suffers from a lack of identity. It is no longer possible to define the big issues as labor-management relations, communism vs. democracy, "big government" vs. "little government." The enemy is more difficult to define.

For several years there has been in Greenwich Village a worthy civic group called "Save the Village" which was organized when city planners seemed bent on leveling everything in sight. It did a wonderful job of alerting the community, helping people who were faced with eviction, and urging the preservation of certain kinds of buildings. It played a significant role influencing the public and politicians in the area. However, I could not tell for the life of me whether that organization was liberal or conservative. We are for "saving the Village," but how we will keep it as it is, and at the same time build enough housing to rent at prices people can pay, is another question. We talk a lot about aesthetics and architectural scale (and I submit that this is practically impossible to label as Democratic or Republican) but whose aesthetics—ours or those of the people who so desperately need a place to live they don't care whether it's genuine brownstone or Greek Doric? Are people who want better aesthetics and planning and less housing liberal or conservative and should they be in the Democratic or Republican parties?

What I am trying to suggest here is that the doctrinaire in politics is dead, but often politicians, parties, and movements don't know it, and the attempts to keep alive bravura radicalism or to judge political personages and issues on the basis of liberal shibboleths or conservative slogans do not serve the good of the political process. Rather, political thought and action must take place where the community problems are— those prosaic and necessary questions of school costs, municipal services, urban sprawl and the like. These kinds of problems will probably not be met by partisan politics alone nor will solutions come by sloganeering causes and crusades.

The elusiveness of the right cause, the clear issue, the ideal party tends to dry up our enthusiasm and stifles our political initiative. Chastened by the knowledge that this cause or that political change will not change the world or perhaps even achieve the justice or the good that we would like, people retreat from the political action that would involve us deeply in the life of our community.

The foregoing seems evidence enough that politics must take on new dimensions if it is to survive as an instrument of the people for the carrying out of public policy. In the evolution of politics there must obviously be revolutionary changes in the structure and shape of political life commensurate with the rapidly changing nature of all our life and culture. It is obvious, for example, that Model T politics in a space age is obsolete. The image of the nineteenth-century ward heeler getting jobs for immigrants and handing out Christmas baskets to the poor is a little incongruous in the mid-twentieth century where neighborhoods might take on the complexity which even cities did not possess a hundred years ago. (More people live in the area of East Harlem than in the whole city of New Haven.)

However, not only the structures of politics (the way in which political decisions are related to public interests and needs), but the presuppositions of politics, which basically define its true nature, must be reexamined in the light of contemporary situations. I would like to discuss some of these dimensions and illustrate, by concrete examples, their relevance in political life in our nation today.

The first dimension is the recognition that the preeminent purpose of all political parties and action is not self-preservation, primarily, but the attainment of a better society or community where justice is tempered by love, freedom by order, and the conflict of diverse interests is ameliorated and adjusted. This proposition suggests among other things the contingent nature of political parties and movements. Political parties or "clubhouses" or reform movements cannot exist for themselves—they are, simply, social and public instruments for the purpose of securing certain goals and objectives for the community or state and nation, goals which are usually stated in religious and moral terms or the terminology of human values.

No political club (or leader) or action is an end unto itself

—in politics ultimate allegiance must always be somewhere else. One writer has suggested that not only the most religious but the most *political* statement in the whole Bible is the commandment in Exodus: "I am the Lord your God, who brought you out of the land of Egypt, out of the house of bondage. You shall have no other gods before me." This means for the political leader that he recognizes that his authority and power, as well as the authority and power of his political government or party, rest upon higher authority.

Lenin, the architect of Communism, was logically right when he said if *political ends* were to be supreme, religion must be wiped out or made subservient to the state.

Max Weber, the sociologist, draws a distinction between two ways of making politics a vocation: "either one lives for politics or one lives off politics." But I think in both instances one assumes a false posture and treats politics as an end in itself. It is true of reform political clubs as well as of intrenched regulars who exist solely for the sake of the spoils system. Many who launch a vigorous reform movement in the name of the community's good, the righting of social wrongs, end up so enamored of the game of politics that they have no time to devote to the basic tasks for which the political movement was called into being.

Another significant dimension is that political parties and leaders must possess an adequate and realistic anthropology and sociology as they seek and use their power to influence and govern. First, in regard to realistic anthropology—the political leader's views on human nature vitally affect his public philosophy. I for one want to be sure that there is a recognition by a political leader of the limitations and distortions occasioned by our human egocentricity which affects all human beings in the use of their power and reason. Our judgment and our decisions are seriously colored by an inordinate self-interest which continually blinds us to the interests of others. In all of us truth is twisted by our own insecurities and our incomplete grasp of reality. "The power we reach for in our weakness corrupts us; the truth we search for in our ignorance is twisted to our own purposes; the goodness with which we cover up our self-centeredness makes hypocrites of us all." The way this truth about men affects the political state is summed up cogently by Reinhold Niebuhr in his *Children of Light and the Children of Darkness:*

. . . no matter how wide the perspectives which the human mind may reach, how broad the loyalties which the human imagination may conceive, how universal the community which human statecraft may organize, or how pure the aspirations of the saintliest idealists may be, there is no level of human, moral or social achievements in which there is not some corruption of inordinate self-love . . . there is no historical reality whether it be church or government, whether it be reason of wise men or specialists which is not involved in the flux and relativity of human existence, which is not subject to error and sin, which is not tempted to exaggerate its errors and sins when they are made immune to criticism.

When this view is not considered, the way is laid open to political chauvinism and the transforming of political campaigns into moral crusades. I remember being a part of one reform movement that continually accused the regular incumbent machine of not understanding nor really believing in the rights of minority groups, but do you know it was next to impossible for that reform group to scare up one or two members of a minority group as window dressing for their own movement. Little wonder that one of the exclamations of the sensitive Negro is, "God save us from the liberals and the reformers!"

Many good reformers tacitly assume that the basic reason for changing the leadership of government is because of those "bad guys" in there who should be replaced by incorruptible and high-principled men. If they do not believe this, I can dismiss it as campaign rhetoric; if they do, it belies a basic naïvete about human nature and I would not want to trust them with political power. A reformer would be much more honest and realistic if he admitted that his nature is corruptible, too, and because this is so, promise to keep open the channels of checks and balances, the democratic dialogue between electorate and elected, so that his decisions may be subject to the will of the people. This is the danger of all one-party nations, states and cities like Russia, and Mississippi and New York City—unchallenged and uninterrupted power builds illusions of divinity in ordinary human beings.

The concomitant to the foregoing is an adequate and realistic view of society. Society is a complex organism built on certain mutuality of interests and organized to defend those interests against disorder from within or threats from without. Man exists in the midst of this complex of relationships upon which he depends for the physical and psychological necessities of life. Because he is a limited and dependent creature, and unable to see the complete whole (and because of the self-esteem we mentioned), he is always making relative judgments about his rights and duties in the midst of these complex relations.

The task of politics is to help balance these rights and duties with individual freedom in the social order.

A third dimension is that there must be a restoration of the true and deep relationship of ethics and politics. Their complete divorce in recent times has led to a serious crisis. We are not talking here about the instillation of morality into every political issue so that it becomes a crusade. Max Weber, in his sociological essays on *Politics as Vocation,* argues for an "ethics of responsibility." He says that:

The matter does not appear to me so desperate if one does not ask exclusively who is morally right and who is morally wrong, but if one rather asks: Given the existing conflict, how can I solve it with the least internal and external danger for all concerned?

Such is not possible unless there is a consensus among contend-
ing groups to respect each other's right to continue in the
society. This requires that we see compromise in the frame-
work of some kind of "ethics of responsibility" and not as the
result of amoral politics. *Compromise is to political action what
tolerance is to religion.* Because there are basic and significant
differences between religions, tolerance is a very important
factor; and because in politics there are two viable sides to a
political issue, compromise is an important stance. It is when
compromise is seen as betrayal, and mediation is interpreted
as treason, that dialogue disintegrates in our political life.

This occurs at every level of political action, but let's illustrate in the area of international relations. Many times, for
example, we are victims of our own propaganda when the
State Department, finding it expedient to negotiate with Communist nations, discovers it has been rendered largely impotent
by the propaganda which labeled its opponent as satanic
while picturing the United States as so "morally clean." It
appears to the American public that the State Department is
entering into negotiations with the devil himself. We then witness our propaganda agencies undertaking a whitewash job
to convince the public and Congress that these are fit people
to keep company with. Thus the citizens of this country are
tempted to oscillate between two pictures of their opponents
in the struggle: one cynical, one illusory, both dangerous.

An "ethics of responsibility" in political life would not lead
us to moralistic crusades nor tempt us to resort to demonology
in dealing with our opponents. For this ethic has reconciliation
as its good.

Without some attention given to these dimensions in the
political movements of our time, there can be no real reforma-
tion and reshaping of the political process—all the way from
the election district to the Presidency. But to talk of what is
missing in our political life is not to let us off the hook, for we

cannot escape so easily by taunting the imperfections and hypocrisy of political institutions. We must be keenly aware that we are morally responsible for the acts and defaults of our politicians. The fact that we have delegated the job of feeding the hungry, clothing the naked, and sheltering the homeless does not free us of our responsibilities, nor can we free ourselves by pleading the remoteness of these acts.

There is a desperate need for public-spirited persons in the building and reshaping of the political parties of our land. We have plenty of people with drive, ambition and self-interest in politics, but we are short on people dedicated with real selflessness to the public's good and to political reform. True reform is a long, difficult task requiring both passion and perspective and the deep conviction to back it up. All phony insurgency and mock liberalism wither and die under the long and tedious haul of making democratic and responsible instruments out of political parties and movements. There is one sure law we can count on in a society where there is government by the consent of the governed—the public (you and I) will get the kind of politics and the kind of government we deserve. It is devoutly to be desired that these times of crisis will find us deeply concerned about participation in the essential dialogue of democracy inherent in the political process.

The Fourth Man

Some Reflections on the Revolutionary Changes in the Style of Being Human

THERE WAS A provocative essay written in 1952 by a Dutch historian named Hoekendijk who suggests that it is possible in modern times to discern in the evolution of human consciousness a new type of person—one whom he calls "the fourth man." This "fourth man" supersedes the three types already produced in Western culture, namely, Christian man, the Renaissance individualist, and the bourgeois moralist. In short, the fourth man will be post-Christian, post-individualist, and post-moralist. Whether or not one can agree with this depiction of a new kind of "man" evolving in our times, I think it does prove that the major crisis of our time is a crisis in the human person. It has only been about a hundred years since Nietzsche declared "God dead" and set man free from his supernatural moorings. And I am not at all sure that we see clearly what has happened to him in his "emancipation." It is much easier for us to detect the change of fashions in what we wear, or the style of architecture, than to notice the revolutionary changes in what it means to be human. This is particularly so in America where our affluence insulates and isolates us from the world. I wonder if we feel the full impact of the crisis. Are we really aware of a steady rehumanization of persons that has gone on apace in the past century? It was easy for Nietzsche to see that "God is dead," but I wonder if the demise of man, as we know him, will be as easily evident or proclaimed with such bravado.

We believe that man is mechanized and degraded only in totalitarian countries and not in our country. Menotti in his opera *The Consul* tells such a story: John Sorel, the hero of a struggle for freedom, flees his country for safety. His wife Magda knows that he cannot return to her and their child; she must join him. She tries to see the Consul who can permit her to join her husband, but she gets only as far as the secretary:

MAGDA: I must see my John and you, only you, can help me. May I speak to the Consul?
SECRETARY: I give you these papers. This is how to begin: Your name is a number. Your story's a case. Your need a request. Your hopes will be filed. Come back next week.
MADGA: And will you explain to the Consul?
SECRETARY: But what is there to explain?
MADGA: Explain that John is a hero . . . explain that the web of my life has worn down to one single thread, and the hands of the clock . . . glitter like knives. Explain to the Consul! explain!
SECRETARY: But what is there to explain?
MAGDA: Explain that John is a hero, explain that he's *my* John! Explain to the Consul. Tell him *my* name. Tell him *my* story. Tell him *my* need!
SECRETARY: Fill in these papers. This is how to begin: Your name is a number. Your story's a case. Your need a request. Your hopes will be filed. Come back next week.

As frustration mounts on frustration, Madga finally cries out:

If to them, not to God, we now must pray
tell me, Secretary, tell me
who are these men?
If to (men), not to God, We now must pray,
tell me, Secretary, tell me
Who are these dark archangels?

The parable of this opera doesn't concern just the workings of a dictatorship. It tells us of the crisis in the human person, and we must be aware that the forces at work in modern society are combining to shape and misshape all our images of what man really is. Some years ago, P. S. Richards, anticipating this differently, said: "The question is no longer whether we can believe in God, but whether or in what sense we can believe in man." In other words, what is *human* about a human being? What do I see when I see a man?

Before we turn to the plight of the "fourth man," let us look a moment at the image of man so prevalent today. One textbook used in our American colleges contains the following definition: "a human being is an ingenuous assembly of portable plumbing." What a glorious distinction! The 11th edition of the *Encyclopaedia Britannica* contains another noble definition. It says, "man is a seeker after the greatest degree of comfort for the least necessary expenditure of energy." Well, these are amusing, but they are a long way from defining what a human being is. The most revealing images are probably those found in literature and philosophy.

We will discover in contemporary literature naked, naturalistic man devouring himself in narcissistic gluttony, sucking every sensation from experience, robbing every moment and every person of all that it can give him, here and now. This is hedonistic man, and the image is the same whether it is the eye-patched Dapper Dan of "distinction-ads" who is part of the Cadillac society and lives off others, or the nonconforming, bearded "beat" who lives in his bare pad and feeds on himself. For both, life is a set of appetites to fill, a lot of thirst to quench, a lot of experiences to feel.

Take John Osborne's *Look Back in Anger* that opens up the exposed nerve ends of the younger generation in Britain and lets us hear their *real* cries of defiance and indignation at the world bequeathed them. Despite all our sympathy and identification with these people, I think we have to agree with Tom Driver's appraisal of Osborne's view of the human being. He observes in *The Christian Century:*

The play is clearly the story of subhumans . . . it is the story of a deliberate regression into screeching primitive, yet passionless existence. The play contains some talk of religion, church and parsons but its environment far from being one with no hope for redemption is one in which redemption could have no conceivable meaning. Men in hell may be set free. Squirrels in dreys neither wish for nor receive any salvation. John Osborne's characters are in a desperate flight out of the pain of being human into anesthesia.

Perhaps the existentialists in our time come close to defining what it means to be human. They say that the essential thing that can be said about man is that he is an *"existing self or person."* This is to say that man's inmost reality—his being or self or "I"—transcends the external world with which he is always involved and also transcends the inner world of his subjective feelings and experience.

This existential anthropology also claims that man is a *uniquely historical being* whose historicity, as Heidegger puts it, is either "authentic" or "unauthentic." To be a man is to be continually confronted with *decision,* a situation caused by one person's encounter with other persons and with destiny. This tremendously significant fact of our interpersonal relationship we have not fully grasped. To know and understand the mysterious power of "meeting" another person I think is sometimes beyond us. A meeting must be without fear or reserve; one must present one's naked self, and similarly one must seek the real self in the other. One must have no ulterior motive, such as the desire to teach, to influence, to control; one's only desire must be to meet the other and speak the word which expresses one's whole being. One's demand of the other must be: Be yourself—don't imitate me or anyone else; do not hide yourself under a mask of politeness. Meeting will often be combat, for it means facing the challenge of the other, but out of such combat may come re-creation. To be a real person—to be human—means to know such encounter, to experience the other self who stands over against my self and know that in some measure I am completed by that other, is to experience a genuine human feeling.

Whether this "fourth man" is a species we have met in concretion or only exists in some kind of phenomenological sense, he may be a future type. Increasingly, he does seem to be the hero or protagonist of much contemporary literature. He also keeps turning up as our roommate, or the colleague at the office or the fellow at the club. He does seem real to many people. Before we describe "the fourth man," one small disclaimer is necessary. From a sociological point of view, it may seem far too much of a generalization, when there are so many social types of man, to discuss one specific type. But at the risk of incurring the wrath of scientific sociologists, I must at least point to what seems to be the emergence of a new type of man. I don't believe he is confined to American culture by any means, but perhaps he is a product or mutation of the Western world.

What are the marks of "the fourth man"? Does he have any special characteristics that set him apart? While they are not utterly unique, some impress one. Earlier we spoke of a world of "cosmic disturbances" and of man being dislocated in space —dislocation is in many ways an apt description of our man. Sometimes this dislocation may be interpreted as disorientation. Part of his displacement is that of identity—he is the "nameless one." Most of the time he doesn't know his true name, nor is there any meaning in the name by which he is called. Historically one's name was a very significant thing; a name was that by which the person was summoned into the world of thought and was necessary to his full existence; it said something important about his nature.

I am reminded of a piece by Adam Margoshes in *The Vil-*

lage Voice a few years ago about his first name. He wrote:
"My first name—you could hardly call it my Christian name—
was Zion. My parents' excuse for this abomination was that I
was born in the year of the Balfour Declaration. It was also
the year of the Russian Revolution and I actually had school-
mates named Lenin and Trotsky. Adam is my inside name. I
gave it to myself when I was twenty." Names today have
little to do with identifying who we are and where we belong.

This sense of dislocation in "the fourth man" indicates that
he has no homeland, and his exilic nature seems to be a dominant motif in his life. Like the children of Israel in Babylonian
captivity, commanded to sing their song in a strange land, he
can no longer remember the tune or the words or why they
meant something to him. He has wandered from the homeland of his heritage and has severed the roots with the past
in an act of emancipation that is more like self-mutilation.
He has successfully (at least in his conscious life) cut himself
off from the past. His soul has no fatherland, his spirit no
community of identification; and he is postmodern cosmopolite
without a history. As Gertrude Stein might put it: "The deracinated Jew is like the deracinated Negro is like the deracinated
European is like the deracinated American." His roots with
the past successfully obliterated, the future mushroom clouded
with uncertainty, this man, perhaps more than any of his
predecessors, lives in and for today.

He is also exiled from his family which gave birth to and
nurtured him. He may yet practice the polite family amenities,
such as visits on the holidays or birthday cards, but there are
no real roots that link him to the family. He sometimes pretends it's not true that—to use the title of Thomas Wolfe's
book—*You Can't Go Home Again,* and he goes back to see
the familiar landmarks, but it's different and strange somehow, and he senses the difference and nothing can be done

about it. Whether because of the structured mobility of society or by self-motivated flight, he broke the tie that bound him to family—the mutuality of interests, concerns and commitments. Or perhaps it came in the sharp violence of open conflict, or perhaps he drifted away in a silent misunderstanding. However it happened, one day it was gone and a mysterious loneliness sprang up amid comfortable companionship, and his life was set in different paths. The family is scattered in all the world with nothing to bind their dismembered parts together. The loss of these roots with the family is part of his dislocation in the world.

In his displaced home and foreign land there is no ritual. I am not talking about the neglect of ecclesiastical rites and liturgies. I am talking about the communal ceremonies and celebrations that play such an important role in making our history as selves significant—those polestars of sanctitude in time and space which gave to man those deeper approbations for existence, and kept alive in people a sense of the mysterious and transcendent ground of life. In the world of the "fourth man," culture is de-ritualized, and the sense of wonder is gone out of life. Before the mechanization and technical efficiency of his collective life, all the solemn occasions and sacred calendars go down, and little that is meaningful replaces them. R. H. MacIver says in *Authority and the Individual:* "No ceremonies salute the time clock and the steam whistle, no hierophants unveil the mysteries of the counting house, no myths attend the tractor and the reaper-binder, no dragons breathe in the open hearth furnace. For millions the art of living is detached from the business of living and must find what refuge it can in the lengthened interval between today's work and tomorrow's." This postreligious man is emancipated from the pomp and circumstance of superstition, from the trappings of medieval mummery, only to be enslaved by a crass mediocrity and a devastating routine of distraction to hide the heartache of his "homesickness" in this world between the ages.

This emerging archetype of man also is suffering from desensitized emotions and the dulling of awareness and empathy. A character in Jules Romains' novel, *Verdun: Men of Good Will*, about World War I describes this best:

I sometimes find myself wondering in a sudden panic, whether I'm not in the way of developing great numb patches in my sensibility of which I shall never be cured—even if I do come through this war . . . Shall I ever again know what delicacy of feeling is? I may be nervous, irritable, exasperated by trifles, but shall I ever recover that sensitiveness which is the mark of civilized man? I sometimes see myself in the future transformed into a sort of invalid who has suffered an amputation of all . . . his fingers and can only feel things with a couple of stumps. And there will be millions of us like that.

What an amazing prediction come true. Here we are "spiritual amputees" of the twentieth century deformed by the totalitarian terrorism of post-World War I and the devastation of a second global conflict. The events of the present have completed the desensitizing process until our emotions are immune to the most horrible atrocities and violence and crimes against human beings. I am not arguing that man is more evil or brutal than he was in 700 B.C. but simply suggesting that perhaps now more than any other time in the modern period he seems able to view incidents of unbelievable inhumanity and seemingly be unmoved. However, even more foreboding is his ability to discuss rationally and with a disgusting detachment the possible justification for moral outrages against humanity. He can rationalize or dismiss in one breath the Buchenwalds, the Hiroshimas and the Budapests of this world without a raised eyebrow or a stammer on his lips.

Some cultural analysts call this a defense mechanism to preserve one's sanity in an insane world of brutal violence and irrational misconduct. By playing it "cool," one is able to stifle the passionate protest that cries to be heard, to protect the heart from fatal wound or aching hurt.

On the other hand it could be a more serious malady. The cruelty and terror of these times could have shell-shocked the emotions and buried the feelings by which humans reach out to each other and have produced in its place men of cold reason and calculated conduct. As Paul Elmen puts it: "Men not even looking through the window to watch a Rembrandt paint, not even caring when Ibsen brought out a new play, not even saddened when Sacco and Vanzetti died." In order to be immune to the "slings and arrows of outrageous fortune," man becomes inoculated against the love of life and compassion for humanity. He is willing to sell the uncertainty of a passionate conviction for the soundness of a rational explanation, to trade the irrationality of tragedy of an uncertain present for the safety of a planned and guaranteed future, to trust the reasoned efficacy of the mind rather than the throbbing passion of the heart that recoils before human indignity; he chooses to be the Captain Vere rather than Billy Budd.

The more one sees this species of detached man, with his uncanny ability to explain and justify both the illogical good and the barbaric evil in this life, it makes one long for the uncautious, fanatical person of the "true believer," unwise in his overzealous surety, but alive with his passionate belief. But perchance never again will men be able to believe with such certainty and therefore never able to feel with such sensitivity and emotion. Then it is logical to conclude that it is precisely this man, with his sensitivity amputated, who is finally, under pressure, capable of inhuman excesses.

Also, in the midst of this world of "the fourth man," there is a *disintegration of vital communication,* and it plagues the deeper levels of all his personal interrelationships. Remember Eliot, speaking about the estranged husband and wife in *The Cocktail Party,* saying: "They make noises and think they are talking to each other. They make faces and think they understand each other and I am sure they don't." This is the state of mankind today, and it permeates every realm of life. Isn't it ironic that in an age where technologically the art of communication transmission has been extended to worlds as yet unknown, we should be deprived as individuals of true communication? We have done the Tower of Babel fanatics one better; we have bounced our gossip off the galaxies and received our own whispers back. Would that we had some meaningful message for the other worlds! We are living in the most verbose of all ages with very little to say. In gigantic steps of scientific improvement, we harness the airwaves and fill the wavelengths with banality and triviality. We are overwhelmed by words, but words in an age of mass communication tend to be hollow reflections of the very person one is talking to. Precisely because they are empty, words bounce back and forth, never touching the persons involved and never revealing their inmost souls. This is true of the much talked about "dialogue" in our time.

Did we not hold out hope that the revolutionary new means of communication would enhance our understanding of ourselves and the world we live in? We felt if we could know about others and they about us, it would halt the fast-moving breakdown of communication. Let's take an illustration from the most powerful media of our culture—radio and TV—and their influence on us. (Incidentally, according to recent statistics, we as a nation devote more time to mass-produced communication than to paid work or play or anything except sleep.) TV alone, only fifteen years old as a mass media, demands one-fifth of the American waking hours. As communicators, we are being displaced by receiving sets (just like the science-fiction writers predicted). Because the speaker and the tube speak in our place, they gradually deprive us of the power of speech, thus transforming humans into passive dependents.

Dr. Gunther Anders, speaking of the effects of radio and TV on Americans, says that as a result of broadcasting, everything is brought to use—the mountain to the prophet, the world to man—and this is bound to have important repercussions. Even if these implications are one-sided and are not balanced by positive contributions, still they are sobering enough to elicit serious reflection. Dr. Anders says first that when the world comes to us instead of our going to it, we are no longer "in the world" but only listless, passive consumers of the world; we wait for the events of the world to be shown us, like the next commercial on TV. Secondly, since the world comes to us only as an image, it is half present and half absent—in other words, phantomlike. This is part of the burden of Daniel Boorstin's thesis in *The Image* which claims that when you continually live on a diet of secondhand experiences—pseudo-events and packaged personalities; you soon fail to distinguish between reality and appearances in the world. Thirdly, when the world is only perceivable but no more than that (i.e. not subject to our action), we are all transformed into "eavesdroppers" and "peeping toms." The implications of these brief challenges certainly deserve more discussion and are only suggestive. The fact remains that methods and means of communication (however perfected) are never guarantees that men will better be able to communicate and therefore understand one another.

There are some who say that the disintegration of communication comes primarily because we have lost our common language—a general semantics. All words mean different things to different people.

How precariously peace and war depend upon words was frightfully illustrated several years ago when Mr. Mikoyan appeared on "Meet the Press" and faced a barrage of pointed questions from American reporters. Even with the help of a splendid interpreter, those men passed each other like ships in the night until, in the last frustrating minutes of that proliferation of words, one correspondent asked the ultimate question: How can there be understanding and goodwill between our countries when we use the same words for different meanings? This illustration on TV was a reenactment of what is happening over and over in the broad field of human relations.

In the contemporary theater, men like Ionesco and Beckett have introduced the "drama of noncommunication." If you remember that dramatic final eclipse of speech in the last act of *Rhinoceros* where Berenger speaks:

I can't bear the sound of them any longer, I'm going to put cotton wool in my ears. The only solution is to convince them—but convince them of what? Are the changes reversible, that's the point? Are they reversible? It would be a labour of Hercules, far beyond me. In any case, to convince them you'd have to talk to them and to talk to them I'd have to learn their language. Or they'd have to learn mine. But what language do I speak? What is my langauge? Am I talking French? Yes, it must be French. But what is French? I can call it French if I want and nobody can say it isn't —I'm the only one who speaks it. What am I saying? Do I understand what I'm saying? Do I?

Berenger's plight is that of man today, condemned by the breakdown of language to silence and solitude.

"The fourth man" *lives almost entirely off social structures and institutions that give his life meaning*—his individual and personal nature seems robbed. Perhaps because of all the ways technological and impersonal mass culture has helped obliterate individuality and personal identity, men have clung like straws in the wind to any hope that promised to give them meaning and in some measure define their purpose for being. In a world of supragroups and institutions within institutions,

man has settled for the issuance of his identity card of existence by the social institutions which create the many public
selves he is or roles he plays.

Look at him as he lives out his many lives. At the break-
fast table he is the meek and dutiful husband cowed by his
wife and intimidated by his children; he catches the 8:02, and
in the club car he is transformed by his new social environment into a bundle of loudmouthed bravadoes about financial
wizardry on Wall Street, the unmerciful "put-down" of his
closest business rival, and the almost successful conquest of
his new secretary; an hour or so later he is the reserved, conservative junior executive of Chemicals Unlimited; at lunch
he is the buoyant, backslapping Babbitt of the Rotarians; at
the 5 o'clock cocktail party he is the debonair, sophisticated
bon vivant of the martini set; that evening in a meeting in his
community church, he is a mixture of pious humility and
mawkish sentimentality; at home later in his own living room
he is the apogee of quiet boredom, wondering which one of
the proliferation of social selves is really he. Will the *real*
John Doe please stand! And the tragedy is that no one does!

This is not another unreasoned castigation of role-playing
in this life; it is I believe a necessary part of our social existence; however, it is one thing to take roles, and it is quite
another to allow those social institutions in which we live to
create or misshape our individual beings completely. Our
"fourth man" seems to be swallowed by these structures. Peter
Berger, the author of *The Precarious Vision,* an analysis of
the social fictions by which we organize life, has a critical
word to say: "The social sciences present us not so much
with man as slave as with man as the clown. The precariousness of personal identity in society is to be seen as the result,
not so much of iron bondage but of the dramatic necessities of
the stage. It is true that, like the physical man, social man is
a most sensitive creature. Just a little more cold, a little more

heat and man dies on the spot. Just a little social rebuff, a couple of picayune failures, and the precious construction of self-esteem and self-respect falls to pieces."

The landscape of our present society is strewn with the bodies of innumerable such casualties usually safely hidden in hospitals for the mentally ill, another of society's institutions for the rehabilitation of social fatalities. Our postmodern man seems to have taken the social structures of his age too seriously (he should not deny their reality but put them in human perspective), and has allowed them to determine completely his individual identity. Perhaps he was forced to do this by an obsessional longing for something which would give shape and validity to his personal individuality.

This "fourth man" is one for whom all the old beliefs hold no meaning. Archibald MacLeish talks about ours as an "age where all the metaphors have died." "The fourth man" is not only post-Christian, in that the creeds and beliefs of that faith are meaningless for him, but he is postreligion in that all the symbols and myths of religious faith appear powerless to make his world meaningful or to provide a frame of reference for any values or morality that are more than shifting sand. The institutional religious life of America has done little to halt the onrushing progress toward a beliefless world for today's man. All the forms of American religion have seemed only to reinforce the fact that faith appears either impossible or irrelevant in a time "of belief in the death of God." We are reminded in the novels of Camus, Kafka and Koestler that it is not only a world where the false gods and the phony idols of ideology have perished, but where the holy God of Judeo-Christian tradition has also disappeared, withdrawn from the world and our experience—and the word *God* receives back nothing but an echo from the vacuum of man's unbelief. It is of little comfort to hear the "statistical optimism" of religious leaders whistling in the dark as they walk through

the cemetery where men are "howling over the grave of God."
It would be more wholesome for these leaders, rather than
trying to prolong a spurious revival of religion, to take cog-
nizance of how much men miss God. But then it does take
courage to confess that we live in an age of disbelief—where
men are not deprived of the desire but only the capacity for
belief.

This was brought strongly to mind recently when the Judson
Poets Theatre in New York produced the York Mystery Plays
on the Nativity. One perceptive critic reviewing the play
said:

It is no simple thing to witness the mystery plays today, bringing to
them as we do the corruption of all our knowledge. Today it is
hard for us to know what stands behind the figures of the mysteries; we come like tourists observing tribal rites; we see patterns
but do not feel the blood. It is pointless then to ask how we are to
view the mysteries, for we bring to them what we have become
and what we cannot unlearn. Given this myopic disbelief, it is possible to appreciate the patterns but not possible to get at the center
of things.

Though this "fourth man" may be freed from the faith in
a God of life who delivers and redeems, he has not been
concomitantly freed from the "powers" and "demons" that
dominate his existence. At one time he experienced these
powers as the dark princes of the underworld, the magical
demons that possessed and terrorized his life. Today these
powers have simply changed their names; they are "bloods,"
"nation," "class," "statistical possibilities" and all the other
"fates" by which man is deprived of his freedom and personal
responsibility. What this man seems to long for is, as one
writer has put it, "someone to de-fatalize him" and liberate
him from the collectivities and powers so that he may control
them for his own good. No deus ex machina will do the job;
no metaphysical or doctrinal system, existential or otherwise
will be acceptable to him. If religious institutions continue to

think in these terms, they will prove utterly impotent. The only thing he is capable of receiving and utilizing is a sense of a posture in life, a style of living and acting that is a way of belonging in the world. It is born of a radical freedom.

We have been describing the possible emergence of a new type of human being in Western culture. It is possible that he is only a figment of the sociologist's imagination; but on the other hand it is altogether possible that we find his traits in ourselves, already here, in embryonic stages. Will he be an improvement on his predecessors? Will he be a dangerous man? It will all depend on what he finds to believe in, how much hope and vision he is able to salvage from the cataclysms that have shaken his world. It seems clear that he will avoid the illusions and exaggerations of his three progenitors, but only if he has learned some hard lessons about what makes for his true humanity will he be saved from creating gigantic new deceptions to cover his failure at being human.